how to have
a good
death

An Endemol Production as seen on BBC2

*This book is dedicated to all those individuals and families
who contributed their thoughts and described their experiences
in order that others might achieve a good death.*

Esther Rantzen

how to have
a good
death

preparing and planning, with informed
choices and practical advice

foreword by Esther Rantzen

A DORLING KINDERSLEY BOOK

LONDON, NEW YORK, MUNICH, MELBOURNE, DELHI

Project Manager and Editor Debbie Beckerman
Senior Editor Dawn Henderson
Managing Art Editor Heather McCarry
Managing Editor Julie Oughton
Production Controller Liz Cherry
Art Director Peter Luff
Operations Publishing Manager Gillian Roberts
Publisher – Special Projects Stephanie Jackson
Publisher Corinne Roberts

First published in Great Britain in 2006 by
Dorling Kindersley Limited
80 Strand, London WC2R 0RL

A Penguin Company

2 4 6 8 10 9 7 5 3 1

By arrangement with Endemol UK Productions
Endemol logo © Endemol UK Productions
Endemol Production Team
Presenter and Executive Producer Esther Rantzen
Executive Producer Sara Ramsden
Senior Producer/Director Elizabeth McIntyre
By arrangement with the BBC
BBC logo © BBC 1991
The BBC logo is a registered trademark of the British
Broadcasting Corporation and is used under licence.

Printed and bound by
Printer Portuguesa, Portugal

Discover more at
www.dk.com

Contents

Consultants

Dr Simon Noble MBBS MRCP Dip Pall Med [author of Chapter 2 and Chapter 3 (except where stated)] Clinical Senior Lecturer in Palliative Medicine at Cardiff University and Honorary Consultant at the Royal Gwent Hospital, Newport. His formative years as a doctor were spent in Cornwall and more recently he worked in South Wales as a specialist registrar.

Dr James Stevenson FRACP FAChPM [author of Chapter 1 (except where stated)] Medical graduate of the University of Queensland and a Fellow of the Royal Australasian College of Physicians. Currently a Clinical Fellow in Palliative Medicine at the Marie Curie Palliative Care Institute, Liverpool.

Professor John Ellershaw MA FRCP [consultant for Chapter 1 and co-author of Chapter 3 (LCP section)] Professor of Palliative Medicine at the University of Liverpool. He is Director of the Marie Curie Palliative Care Institute Liverpool, Medical Director of the Marie Curie Hospice Liverpool, and Clinical Director of Palliative Care, Royal Liverpool University Hospitals. He has written extensively on all areas of Palliative Care Medicine.

Jane Feinmann [author of Introduction, Chapter 4 (except where stated) and Chapter 5 (from How different religions handle funerals and burials section) and Chapter 6 (except where stated)] Freelance writer on health and psychology, contributing regularly to national newspapers and magazines as well as writing books. She has been a volunteer for the Befriending Network, befriending people with terminal illness. She has two grown-up children and lives in London.

Clive Peterson [author of Chapter 4 (Keeping the door open section), Chapter 5 (except where stated) and Chapter 6 (Pre-paid funeral plans section)] With his brother, Bryn, Clive runs Peterson Funerals, based in Cwmbran New Town in Wales. They are members of the National Association of Funeral Directors (NAFD) and the British Institute of Funeral Directors (BIFD). As a 17 year old, Clive helped to arrange the funerals for some of the children who died in the Aberfan disaster in Wales.

Dr David Goldhill MA MBBS MD FRCA EDIC [author of Chapter 1 Intensive Care sections] Consultant in Intensive Care and Anaesthesia, the Royal National Orthopaedic Hospital, Stanmore, and Honorary Reader, University College London. Before that, was a Consultant and Senior Lecturer at the Royal London Hospital and Director of Critical Care at Barts and the London Hospital. Council member of the UK Intensive Care Society, has written widely on critical care topics and is an examiner for the UK Diploma in Intensive Care Medicine and the final anaesthetic examinations.

Deborah Murphy [co-author of Chapter 3 (LCP section)] Directorate Manager, Directorate of Palliative Care, Royal Liverpool University Hospitals. National Lead Nurse, LCP. Associate Director, Marie Curie Palliative Institute, Liverpool.

Claire Henry [author of Chapter 3 (NHS End of Life Care Programme section)] National Programme Director, NHS End of Life Care Programme.

Foreword by Esther Rantzen

I hope you have picked up this book with a feeling of hope, not dread. This is not a pessimistic book, nor a frightening one. True, it contains many factual details, and describes events and emotions which many of us usually avoid thinking about. Death has been described as the last taboo. Like children facing a tough exam, in our hearts we may believe that if we don't think about it in advance, perhaps it will never happen. But of course death is the one inevitability. I believe that the truths revealed in this book will take away some of the terror, the unreasoning fear that can undermine us when we consider our own deaths, or the death of someone we love. **I hope you will find this is a helpful book, and a hopeful one.** If knowledge is power, it will give you power in a situation in which you might otherwise feel helpless.

Those of us who have lived through the experience of coping with the death of someone close to us (and I lost my parents and my husband within five years), know that strange sensation of being carried along by a tide, without knowing quite where or how fast you are going, desperately anxious to ask the right questions and do the right thing, and yet not quite sure what to ask or how to act. **There are no rules. All deaths are different.** Every patient has individual needs. If we get them wrong, or let them down, that failure will become a source of regret and sorrow. It can become a barrier that obscures all the happiest memories. That is why a good death is so important, if we can possibly achieve it. It is the key to remembering a good life.

I hope that health care professionals will also read this book. The message contained in it is that death should not be regarded by them as a failure, but a tremendously important milestone in life, as important as birth. Many doctors and nurses may already be involved in pioneering schemes like the ones described in Chapter 3, which carefully lead patients and those close to them down a pathway in which medical intervention supports but does not invade privacy or interrupt communication. But sometimes, particularly in Intensive Care Units where many of us die, the desire to rescue and save may intrude on those last precious moments. In the last hours of my husband's life I was taken out of his arms so that he could have a blood test. The test had no value at that stage. I was never able to return to his arms.

On the other hand, in other ways my family had the privilege of clear, sensitive communication. For example, my husband was told everything he needed to know in order to say goodbye to us all, and that was crucial to him and to us. So I have a great deal to look back on with pleasure. **It may sound odd, to remember the death of someone you love with pleasure, but palliative care consultants know that is the reward of all their skill and efforts.** They want us to be able to die with dignity, privacy and pain free, surrounded by those we love. That is the aim of this book, too.

Sadly, not all deaths achieve that ideal. The programme that inspired this book was based on the largest ever national survey into the management of death, and it revealed many failures and inequities in end-of-life care. That is why the advice in these chapters may turn out to be crucial to you and those closest to you. But even if things seem to be going wrong, there are steps you can take to put them right.

There are two particular pieces of advice I would pick out from the many contained in these chapters. Firstly, if you think that someone you love is experiencing unnecessary pain or other distressing symptoms, do ask to see a palliative care consultant. These are the doctors who specialise in end-of-life care, and a great deal can be done to alleviate pain without shortening life.

Secondly, we potential patients need to change our own attitudes. We must break down the taboo surrounding death, and discuss our own wishes well in advance with those closest to us. **We need to make our wishes clear, so that our families can fulfil them.** Not just a will, or a living will (and for the sake of the many readers who have not yet written either, formats and instructions can be found in Chapter 6). Why not also borrow a video camera and record your thoughts not only about death, but about life as well? In the course of making the programme "How to Have a Good Death" I interviewed some terminally ill patients, and I know how much comfort and inspiration their families gained from watching and rewatching the film in the days after the patient died.

Finally, may I contribute to this book a poem which in my 40 years as a broadcaster was the most requested piece of writing I ever brought to our television audience, and which was voted the nation's favourite poem. Even if it is not to your taste, it may inspire you to collect together the readings and music you would like included in your own funeral or memorial service. My late husband knew his heart disease was likely to shorten his life, and left me a running order for his memorial service, which enabled me to carry out his wishes, and was the last gift of love I was able to give him.

Esther

Esther Rantzen

Do Not Stand at My Grave and Weep by Mary Frye

Do not stand at my grave and weep,
I am not there, I do not sleep.
I am a thousand winds that blow.
I am the diamond glint on snow.
I am the sunlight on ripened grain.
I am the gentle autumn rain.
When you wake in the morning hush,
I am the swift, uplifting rush
Of quiet birds in circling flight.
I am the soft starlight at night.
Do not stand at my grave and weep.
I am not there, I do not sleep.
Do not stand at my grave and cry.
I am not there, I did not die!

Introduction

Back in the 1980s, medicine seemed to be a never-ending success story. A stream of dramatic breakthroughs in surgery, medication and medical technology meant that doctors had unprecedented power to cure disease and prolong life. It was becoming the norm to stay alive for years, even decades, after a diagnosis of serious illness that would have swiftly carried off parents and grandparents.

What was also becoming clear, however, was that there was a downside to these achievements. Dying had become a failure, an embarrassment that doctors preferred to ignore. And with medical training focused entirely on saving lives, there was no time to teach the gentler skills that helped patients to focus on living as fully as possible until the inevitable happened.

The medical curriculum of the 1980s (and beyond) contained little, if any, training in communication skills, especially the stressful business of delivering "bad" news. The modern doctor learnt to be deliberately vague, or to practise a "ritualised optimism".

Death, it seemed, had become a subject that, if not taboo, was easiest to avoid, for all concerned. All well and good, but from the 1980s onwards, the dying and (some of) their doctors were beginning to complain. It was not that people were being denied life-saving treatment. Up to 40 per cent of health care funding was (and still is) spent in the last year of life, much of it on high-tech interventions in the last few weeks of life.

But for all the funding and expertise, there was growing evidence that the terminally ill frequently spent their final weeks in uncontrolled physical pain and emotional isolation. The hospice movement was a response to these problems: offering holistic, non-interventionist, palliative care for the terminally ill, with emotional and spiritual support taking over from drugs and surgery. Even today, however, only four per cent of people die in hospices. And despite the almost universal preference to die at home (according to a November 2005 ICM poll), well over half the population die in hospital, including 50 per cent of those with cancer and 51 per cent of the elderly.

It is here that change is needed – and is finally happening. This book charts some of the new Government and clinical initiatives that are finally bringing the hospice approach to terminal illness to a local hospital near you. This appears to be badly overdue and much-needed. For many people, death is not unexpected and needs to be managed as well as possible, both for the benefit of the person concerned and for the benefit of the surviving loved ones.

Yet death and dying are too serious and important to leave to the medical profession. To have a good death, it seems, we have to enter the arena ourselves: and that means facing up to difficult truths. It also means being practical, such as writing a will and perhaps planning a funeral, and making an Enduring Power of Attorney that nominates a representative to manage our estate as we draw closer to death.

What's more, it is important to acknowledge that doctors will not necessarily tell you all that you need to know, especially that you are dying. Facing up to the prospect of death may make it easier to engage in a frank discussion with your doctors at the time of being diagnosed with a serious illness. Such a discussion can maintain hope and optimism – yet also makes us face up to the limitations of available treatments and what is and what is not acceptable in terms of resuscitation and life support. It may also cover the preferred place of death or the kind of follow-up care that should be provided for children.

"We die whether we think about death or ignore it completely," points out David Kessler, in his book, *The Rights of The Dying*. "But if we choose to, we can have a say in how we die, where we die and what happens before and after. In so choosing, we take on the responsibility of participating fully in our care and in our deaths."

Chapter 1 **How do people die?**

Death occurs at some time in every form of life. Despite the advances in human scientific knowledge and medical skill, we will not live forever. So what is death and why do we die? The philosophical and spiritual thoughts on this question have been debated for thousands of years and cannot be given an adequate response here. And whilst there are many familiar phrases and sayings that refer to death, it is an event that can be hard to define and even harder to confront or accept. Yet, in order to have a good understanding of why people die, it is important to know how they die. It is also important to know that nowadays, thanks to advances in medical and palliative care, it should be possible for almost every person to have "a good death".

What do "death" and "dying" mean?

At a physical level, death is the moment when the body stops living; when the vital organs that normally work together to make us live, stop working. When it becomes impossible for life to continue, the brain, which controls so many organs and bodily processes, stops sending the signals and impulses required to maintain life. This also includes the impulses that make the brain work.

Without the brain's control, the heart stops beating, which means blood stops flowing throughout the body. Without circulation, oxygen, the most vital of life-sustaining elements, can no longer be carried to all the cells that require it to continue working. This includes the brain itself, so within a few moments of the heart stopping, the brain shuts down and death has occurred. Individual cells throughout the body may take a little longer to stop working but the coordinated function that renders us alive stops when the brain stops. These concepts will be expanded on in the following sections of this chapter.

At a spiritual level, death is far harder to define and will depend on one's own beliefs and understanding.

Why do we die?

Scientifically there has been great advancement in some aspects of this question. Much of this advance concerns the science of genetics and deoxyribonucleic acid (DNA), sometimes referred to as the building blocks of life. It is now understood that DNA plays a very important role, not only in life, but even death. In addition to controlling genetic traits such as eye colour and height, DNA controls how frequently cells divide and regenerate. Beyond this, DNA even controls how long cells can live or how many times they can divide before they are exhausted and die. This is why hair falls out and skin develops wrinkles. It is now understood that cells are programmed to die after a predetermined length of time, even if they survive other injuries or insults that could cause an earlier death. This then affects how long our different organs and ultimately our entire bodies can survive; for this reason phrases such as "dying is part of living" and "we all have to die sometime" really are true.

We can now identify various disease processes or events that lead to death and much of modern medicine's resources go into learning why these events occur and how we can prevent or delay them. Our individual DNA not only determines our eye colour and height but also which diseases we may develop and ultimately how we might die. In the case of cancer, the role of the DNA and genes we inherit is now well understood. While we can inherit some genes that protect us from developing certain types of cancer, other genes can increase our chance of developing cancer and also make the cancer more aggressive and harder to treat.

We are living longer due to many factors such as better disease prevention, through public health measures including better nutrition, sanitation, vaccinations and screening programmes, and safety initiatives to prevent accidental or traumatic death. In addition, there are now better treatments for previously untreatable diseases. But we still die.

Dying in Intensive Care

Dr David Goldhill writes: Death has changed from being a private, religious and spiritual event to being something that commonly occurs in hospital, sometimes with the involvement of aggressive organ support. The Intensive Care Unit (ICU) is where the sickest hospital patients are cared for and about 20 per cent of all deaths occur there. The ICU has more staff and equipment than a normal ward. Intensive monitoring, nursing and organ support are available 24 hours a day. ICU admission is restricted to patients who might benefit from extra treatment and is generally not appropriate for those with little or no chance of survival. Patients near the end of their lives with incurable conditions are not admitted to the ICU. Support such as that provided by a palliative care service or a hospice is better able to care for these patients. About three quarters of ICU patients survive to leave hospital, meaning that one quarter dies, usually on the ICU. By looking at what happens on the ICU, we can explore and better understand the process of death.

Patients on the ICU will typically have one or more organ failures. This means that important organs such as the lungs, heart, liver, kidneys, brain or intestine are not working normally. It might also mean that the patient's blood cannot form a clot, or that they have an overwhelming infection. The usual aim of admitting a patient to the ICU is to provide additional time for treatments to have time to work and for the body's own healing systems to be effective.

Lung failure is one of the commonest reasons for ICU admission. This can be because of diseases such as pneumonia, asthma or bronchitis, which directly affect the lungs. However, almost all critically ill patients will require support for breathing, either because their underlying problem or its treatment affects the lung. It is rare for patients not to require extra oxygen and most will also need the support of a ventilator, a machine that assists or takes over breathing. The heart is also commonly affected and treatment usually consists of ensuring there is enough fluid in the circulation and giving drugs that help the heart to pump more strongly. Most vital organs, if not permanently damaged, will recover given time, as long as they receive a good supply of well-oxygenated blood. This needs both the lungs and heart to be working well. Artificial kidneys are also commonly used if there is short-term, reversible kidney failure. Other treatments include blood products to replace red blood cells, and other cells and chemicals that help the blood to clot. Antibiotics will be given to treat infection, and hormones to replace those that need boosting. Food is given either by a tube into the stomach or directly into the bloodstream if the intestines are not working. Drugs are often given to keep patients sleepy or unconscious, and pain free.

Several things affect the chances of a patient surviving to leave ICU. Obviously the underlying disease or illness is very important. Older, frailer patients are generally at greater risk. The chances of dying are also related to the number of organs that fail and how badly they are damaged. There are also risks in the treatment given. Placing tubes and lines into blood vessels, the lungs and elsewhere can increase the risk of infection and further organ damage, and many of the drugs are powerful with their own risks and complications. It often takes hours or days following ICU admission before the doctors and nurses can be sure whether the patient is likely to survive or to die.

Patients are generally admitted to ICU for one or more of the following reasons –

- they have one or more organ failures: the lungs, heart, liver, kidneys, brain or intestine are not working properly
- their blood may not be able to clot
- they might have an overwhelming infection
- they might benefit from intensive treatment: ICU is not appropriate for patients with little or no chance of survival, nor for those near the end of their lives with incurable conditions.

Treatment in Intensive Care

Dr David Goldhill writes: Although efforts are focused on minimising pain and anxiety, intensive care treatment does involve making patients dependent on machines and potent drugs. Some admissions to Intensive Care are planned, for example, following major surgery. However, most admissions are as an emergency and there is no opportunity to discuss with patients and their loved ones what Intensive Care admission involves. In acute situations, such as trauma, a husband, wife or child can be transformed in a brief time from a healthy person into someone at death's door. Their appearance can change radically. They will be connected to a bewildering array of machines, pumps and monitors, and they will usually have tubes inserted into lungs, bladder, stomach and several blood vessels. They may be bloated from fluid, be covered in bruises and have surgical wounds, dressings and fixations. The patient, and even more so the relatives, can feel threatened and intimidated by all that is going on and can feel stress from the interventions that are essential for survival. The Intensive Care Unit is very busy and relatives are often reluctant to trouble the doctors and nurses for information. Most units will have a quiet room where discussions can be held away from the noise and bustle of the clinical area. When a patient is very sick, the staff will usually ensure that loved ones are aware of the gravity of the situation and the options for treatment that are being considered.

Treatment is only continued if there is a realistic chance of success. For many of those who die there comes a time when it is obvious that further treatment will not work. Because of this, decisions are commonly taken in the ICU before death to either limit or withdraw treatment. At this time very few patients are able to be involved themselves in the decision-making process. Typically such decisions will be made by the doctors and nurses in consultation with relatives and carers. At this stage it is usually obvious to relatives that treatment is no longer working. There is usually adequate time to go to a quiet room to discuss the situation and agree a plan of action. The decision may be to place a time limit on further aggressive treatment, or to agree not to add any further treatments or even to withdraw treatments already being given.

If death is inevitable, the emphasis changes from one of cure to one of comfort. The aim is to provide an appropriate pain-free death, which must acknowledge physical, social and spiritual dimensions.

If death is inevitable, the emphasis changes from one of cure to one of comfort.

Brain stem death

Dr David Goldhill writes: The brain is somewhat different from other vital organs. It is particularly vulnerable to even short periods without an oxygen supply and meaningful life is impossible without brain function. Most patients who die do so because the breathing or circulation fail and eventually the heart stops. In a small proportion, the brain is permanently damaged but other vital organs have not yet failed. A small percentage of these patients remain in what is called a permanent vegetative state. These patients show no signs that their brain can think or understand but their other vital organs continue to function. If given food and water and basic nursing care these patients may well survive for many years. In other patients the lower part of the brain, called the brain stem, is destroyed and they will inevitably die no matter what is done. This is because this part of the brain controls breathing and other vital functions. Simple bedside tests can be used to diagnose brain stem death.

In the UK, the diagnosis of brain stem death requires three steps –

1   The patient must have a reason for suffering irreversible brain damage. Common causes are a head injury after a car crash or fall, or a serious bleed into the brain from a burst blood vessel.

2   Reversible causes of coma must be actively excluded. These include the effects of drugs, alcohol, profound cold or metabolic disturbances.

3   A set of bedside tests to confirm lack of brain stem function. These tests are clearly defined and must be performed twice by at least two experienced doctors. If the diagnosis is made, the patient is deemed to have died at the time the first set of tests was completed. In practice, after two sets of tests have been appropriately carried out, the Intensive Care team caring for the patient will consult with relatives, carers and friends of the patient and arrange to withdraw the remaining treatment. The possibility of transplantation is usually discussed after the first set of tests has been completed.

The biology of death

Dr David Goldhill writes: The cause of death is individual but the body always shuts down in the same way –

- The body is a collection of organs made up of cells. When circulation ceases (and, with that, the delivery of oxygen to the cells and the removal of waste products) some cells become damaged and organs fail.

- When the brain is deprived of oxygen for more than a few minutes, it dies.

- As death approaches, waves of morphine-like chemicals, called endorphins, are released, which blot out anxiety and pain.

- Dying cells in the visual cortex start to fire off signals at random. Although our eyes are shut at this stage, it is as if we are still seeing, which may explain the tunnel of light that people talk about when they are brought back from the brink of death.

- Finally, the brain cells detach from one another, breaking the connections they have made during a lifetime of thinking and remembering. The brain is now dead.
- All remaining body functions now cease.
- In death, every tissue and organ shuts down at its own pace.
- After death, the body will continue making skin cells for several minutes.
- Muscles will live on for hours. Eventually they too will stop.
- As cell after cell ceases activity, our bodies stop generating heat and start to cool to the temperature of the room.

Organ donation

In the UK, a donor transplant coordinator is always available to discuss the process with the relatives. Their job is to tell the relatives about organ donation, to assess the suitability of the donor and to support the family through this difficult decision-making process. If agreement is given, the patient's heart, lungs, liver, kidneys and other vital organs are supported in the patient's body until they can be removed for donation. This is known as a *beating heart donation.* Patients with brain stem death cannot breathe by themselves. If organs are not donated the patient is disconnected from the ventilator and, shortly after, his or her heart will stop.

Patients with brain stem death provide most of the organs that are transplanted. The number of these donors is declining, as fewer young people are dying from severe injury or catastrophic brain haemorrhage. There is a move to obtain more organs from patients who die when their heart stops working. These are known as *non-heart beating donors.* Most of these patients are in ICU and are those in whom continued treatment is judged to be futile and it has been agreed that medical treatment should be withdrawn. Some organs such as kidneys, lungs and liver must be removed within minutes of death. Others such as corneas, bone, skin and heart valves can be donated up to 24 hours or even longer after death.

The process of dying

This is even harder to describe than death itself. While we haven't found a way to permanently prevent death, there are some differences in the way we die compared to the past. We have changed the relative proportions of different causes and particularly the timeframes in which death occurs. It is worth considering these different timeframes and this is expanded below. Although the moment of death can usually be considered to be sudden, the process of dying may be recognised so that death is anticipated anywhere from minutes up to years before the final sudden event. There are many events or changes that can signify that an individual is dying; in some people several of these occur whilst death may occur in others with almost no significant events. A description of the possible changes that occur before death will be provided later in the chapter.

Causes of death

There are many different conditions that cause death and these vary from one country to the next and from one era to the next. The table below lists some statistics for England and Wales in the year 2004. The most common causes of death are from cardiovascular diseases, such as heart attacks and strokes, and cancer. Together these account for nearly two out of three deaths.

Causes of death in England and Wales in 2004

Diagnosis	Number of deaths	Percentage (%)
Cardiovascular (e.g. heart attacks, strokes)	190 771	37.1
Cancer	138 058	26.9
Respiratory (e.g. pneumonia, emphysema)	69 462	13.5
Digestive tract	24 979	4.9
Accidents/trauma/poisoning	17 561	3.4
Nervous system	14 589	2.8
Dementia and psychiatric	14 324	2.8
All other causes	44 241	8.6
Total number of deaths	514 250	100

The timeframe of dying

Death can happen suddenly or can follow a short-term illness or a form of long-term illness. The particular experience and timeframe have a huge impact on the patient and his or her friends and relatives, and on the type of care needed.

Sudden death

Sudden death refers to death that is unexpected or unforeseen. The event is so overwhelming that the body cannot continue to function properly and death usually occurs within a few seconds to a couple of minutes. Some examples of causes of sudden death are listed in the box on p.22. In some of these instances, medical technology now exists, which can save lives if the problem can be recognised and treated immediately. For example, giving adrenaline to someone having an allergic reaction can stop the development of shock and airway obstruction if it is given before the circulation fails. In most situations, sudden death implies that relatives and friends do not have time to prepare for the person's death.

Death from acute (short-term) illness

Acute illness develops over a period of hours to days and can put a massive strain on one or many body systems, potentially leading to death. In Western countries, the most common types of illness that can lead to death acutely include infections and organ failure (heart, kidney, liver or lung failure) where death is slower than sudden death indicated above. The process can be seen to evolve anywhere from several minutes to a few days, and will often be accompanied by a range of symptoms and signs that allow medical staff to make a diagnosis, order various investigations and initiate treatment. Even if treatment is appropriate, the illness may still overwhelm the ability of the individual to survive. Sometimes the failure of one organ places an overwhelming strain on other organ systems even if they were not directly affected by the illness; this is called multi-organ failure and is very difficult to overcome once it starts, even with the most intensive care available. As the person deteriorates, it is often possible to see the changes clearly enough to allow the diagnosis of dying to be made. Eventually, some sudden event happens as described above and the person dies. Unlike sudden death, however, relatives and friends usually have some time to prepare for the person's death, although this may not be more than a few minutes or hours.

Possible causes of sudden death

Brain

Massive stroke	haemorrhage – bleeding
	ischaemia – starvation of blood (blood clot or hardened arteries)
Head injury	with or without bleeding (motor accidents, gunshot injuries)
Toxic brain injury	hypoxia – lack of oxygen (failure of circulation, lung failure)
	hypoglycaemia – lack of sugar (too much insulin)

Heart

Cardiac arrest	myocardial infarction – heart attack
	arrhythmia – electrical circuit failure (inherited, severe biochemical disturbance)
	loss of controlling signal from brain
Cardiac rupture	usually caused by another underlying problem

Lungs and airways

Physical obstruction	choking, swelling from severe allergic reaction, laryngeal spasm (e.g. drowning)
Small airway spasm	severe asthma attack
Failure of muscles of respiration	loss of controlling signal from brain (see above)
Lung collapse	pneumothorax (punctured lung)

Circulation

Massive pulmonary embolism	blood clot in the lung usually seen with deep vein thrombosis

Shock (massive drop in blood pressure preventing blood flow to all organs)

hypovolaemic	massive blood loss, haemorrhage
cardiogenic	heart muscle failure after massive heart attack
	loss of controlling signal from brain (see above)
septic	overwhelming infection
anaphylactic	severe allergic reaction

Death from chronic (long-term) illness

As discussed earlier, people are generally living longer due to a combination of strategies that prevent or at least treat diseases that would previously have caused death at an earlier age. People can now live many years and even decades with some diseases, and these are referred to as *chronic illnesses*. Some people with chronic illness do not die from the illness but from sudden death or an acute cause of death as described above. Chronic illnesses may also cause death and generally follow one of three courses or trajectories –

    1 Slow and steady decline.

    2 Chronic limitations with intermittent serious acute episodes.

    3 Period of reasonable health followed by a relatively acute decline.

People can now live many years and even decades with some diseases, and these are referred to as chronic illnesses.

Slow and steady decline

In some cases, these conditions progress slowly over time and lead to death due to a gradual failure of multiple bodily functions. There may never be a specific event that heralds the start of the illness, rather gradual changes that progress and eventually make it more obvious that the person is dying. Treatments may slow the underlying disease or at the very least help maintain as many of the person's functions for as long as possible. A common example of such conditions is dementia. There comes a time when the combinations of problems make it clear the person with the condition is dying, and often there is a long period of time when the patient and his or her family can prepare for this.

Chronic limitations with intermittent serious acute episodes

With other illnesses, there can be acute exacerbations of the chronic illness that require more intense treatment, and sometimes these episodes can prove fatal. Common examples of this include chronic lung diseases such as emphysema, cardiac failure and HIV/AIDS where episodes may require hospital admission. Even when someone looks severely unwell, the treatment can help them survive the episode and return home again. Over time, it is often recognised that the person is weakened by each episode and recovery may not return him or her to the level he or she enjoyed beforehand. The underlying incurable disease often results in a gradual weakening in between the more acute episodes. This progressive weakness reduces the patient's ability to then survive an acute exacerbation. At any one of the acute episodes, a more severe decline can occur and the person may die. Again, some sudden event occurs resulting in death. Compared to the examples above, the person, as well as his or her relatives and friends, may have months or even years to prepare for death. Despite this, the exact moment cannot be predicted and the moment of death may still come unexpectedly.

Period of reasonable health followed by a relatively acute decline

The most common disease that follows this pattern is cancer. With advances in medical treatments over recent decades, people are surviving many illnesses that were previously fatal. A consequence of this is that there has been an increase in the number of people who now develop cancer and approximately one in three people will develop cancer in their lifetime. As a result, more people now die of cancer than in past decades and a little over one in four deaths in England and Wales are due to cancer.

At times, reports are released using words like "epidemic", which often generate fear. This reporting is unhelpful as it does not acknowledge some important realities. At a very simple level, cancer is an abnormal growth of our own cells, which starts when cells divide wrongly and continue to grow out of normal bodily controls. There are many reasons why this may occur. Cancer can start at any age, but it becomes more likely the longer we live. The reason is that the more often cells divide, the more likely it is for one of those divisions to go wrong and lead to cancer. As we survive years longer from other diseases, our chances of developing a cancer increase.

Cancer is becoming more successfully treated over time so that more people are being cured. Even when cancer can't be cured, more people can be given treatments that delay the progression of cancer for months and even years. Over 50 per cent of all people diagnosed with cancer survive more than five years. In some cancers, the figures are much better. For example nearly 80 per cent of all women with breast cancer survive more than five years, as do over 70 per cent of men with prostate cancer. Some cancers are still difficult to survive such as lung cancer where only 6–8 per cent of people survive over five years from diagnosis. Research into better ways to diagnose and treat cancer will lead to further improvement in survival.

Even though treatment and survival are improving, statistics show more people are dying from cancer because of the total increase in numbers of people developing it. In the past, a diagnosis of cancer often meant that death would occur within a few weeks or, at most, months. In this sense, it was seen as a severe acute illness with few or no treatment options. Because of this, the diagnosis of cancer often results in fear far more than other equally fatal illnesses. The modern reality for many people is that cancer now behaves more like a chronic illness.

Even when cancer cannot be cured, current treatments usually allow people to maintain a good level of health and independence for a period of time until the disease progresses. This period varies between individuals and can be anywhere from a few weeks up to many years. In this time, the person's health may be so good that it is not obvious they even have an illness. It is important for a person with cancer to be able to focus on living even if there might come a time when he or she dies from the illness. When cancer progresses and can no longer be treated, a person's health usually deteriorates over a period of weeks, sometimes months, in a steady and measurable way. There are many different ways this may be shown and some of these will be outlined below. At this time, it becomes clearer that death is approaching, although the exact time is impossible to predict in terms any more accurate than some "weeks" or "months". For people living with incurable cancer, there is often time for them, their relatives and friends to prepare for death. In this way, it is more like a chronic illness than an acute illness or sudden death.

What is palliative care?

There are many definitions of palliative care; it is defined by the World Health Organization as "... an approach that improves the quality of life of patients and their families facing the problems associated with life-threatening illness, through the prevention and relief of suffering by means of early identification and impeccable assessment and treatment of ... problems, physical, psychosocial and spiritual."

In general, the purpose of palliative care is to help people living with life-limiting illness. Although the person may well die from their disease, it is important to realise that being diagnosed with life-limiting illness does not mean the person is *dying* from that moment. Rather, they should be able to live a full and comfortable life for as long as possible. Although some people are only referred to palliative care services in the last days of life, many people live for weeks, months or even years with their life-limiting illness and have needs requiring the specialist help provided by palliative care services throughout this time.

The ideas of "disease" and "sickness" (or "being unwell" or "poorly") are often used to mean the same thing but understanding the differences between these ideas will help clarify some of the most important aims of palliative care and the care of the dying.

Being unwell versus having a disease

It is easy to understand that a person with a disease might feel unwell, just as it is easy to understand that a person with no disease will feel well. But it is not uncommon to meet people that fit into two other categories. Firstly, a person may feel unwell but have no physical disease to find; the cause for their unwellness may not be physical, but rather a condition such as stress or anxiety. Alternatively, it is possible for a person with disease to feel well. Cancer, for example, may not cause any symptoms until it has reached an advanced and incurable stage. Sometimes it is possible to treat the symptoms caused by disease even if the underlying disease can't be taken away. When this treatment is successful the person with the disease can once again feel well. This may even be possible when someone is dying. At the very least, one of the key aims of the care of the dying is to minimise the suffering caused by the advanced disease and its symptoms. This can be considered diagrammatically in the box below.

Differences between being unwell and having a disease

	No disease	Disease
Feeling well	Normal healthy state	Aim of good palliative care or subclinical disease
Feeling unwell	Non-physical condition e.g. stress, anxiety	Commonly seen at some stage with most illnesses

Diagnosing dying

Although the two words "diagnosing dying" may sound simple, this is in fact one of the most difficult challenges in medicine. Medical professionals spend years learning how to assess unwell people, make a diagnosis and then treat them to make them well again. They are trained to become problem solvers; if there is a problem it *must* be fixed, which implies it *can* be fixed. At times even the most unwell person can make a full recovery if treated well.

In most situations, a person who is unwell wants to be made well. Most of us do not want to die if confronted with a life-threatening situation and there is an expectation that treatments should at least be discussed and usually given. Unfortunately, as discussed at the start of this chapter, death will occur in all of us at some time. Even the best treatments in the world cannot stop the natural process of dying, because the problems have become unfixable. However, many of the changes that occur when someone is dying are the same as those that occur when someone is very unwell but still treatable. Some of the changes seen in the dying phase will be discussed shortly.

For the treating doctor it is essential to know not only about the disease affecting the person but also about the person affected by the disease. Understanding where the person has come from with the disease helps determine where the person is going to and therefore if treatment will be appropriate or successful. For the person who has been living with an incurable disease but has been well, it may be entirely appropriate to thoroughly assess and treat him or her if he or she becomes suddenly less well. On the other hand, if someone has been getting less well over time because of a disease that has not responded to treatment and becomes even more unwell then it may be that he or she is now dying and can no longer be treated in any way to prolong life.

To help illustrate the difficulty of separating dying from just being very unwell, a couple of different concepts will be discussed.

Cardiac defibrillators, resuscitation and advanced life support

It is very important to recognise the difference between when a person might die because his or her heart stops beating, and when the heart stops beating because the person is dying. In the first situation, the heart stops because of a specific problem that could cause death if left untreated and therefore might be solved if treated successfully. The person can return to good health. In the second situation, where the person is dying, even if the heart can be restarted there is still no message coming from the brain to allow it to continue. Attempting resuscitation in this situation is not likely to work and may cause suffering at an already difficult time for the dying person and family and friends.

Cardiac defibrillators can reverse life-threatening heart rhythm disturbances through the use of an electric shock and are most successful if that problem exists without other simultaneous issues or if the person can be treated for those issues successfully at the same time. The main purpose of cardiac resuscitation (cardiac massage) is to keep a person's circulation going until the heart rhythm can be restarted by a cardiac defibrillator. In itself cardiac massage does not restart the heart. Advanced life support such as that provided in Intensive Care Units is usually used to support the different body systems through a life-threatening yet reversible situation until the body can work independently again.

In many situations, unsuccessful resuscitation is attempted because the exact history of the person and their disease is not known or fully understood. At other times, it is because the situation has not been fully communicated to the patient or their next-of-kin, and a request for active resuscitation is made in the belief that the problem is fixable. There is also the natural response to want to help someone and a fear that we may let them down if we don't at least try. In reality, there are many situations in which resuscitation is not likely to help the dying person, but help can be provided by simply being there with him or her.

Beneficial treatment versus medical futility

Similarly, yet more complex, it is important to understand the difference between the situation in which someone's life is limited or threatened by death due to reversible problems, and that in which problems develop because the person is dying.

In a person who is not otherwise dying, successful beneficial treatment of the problems will allow recovery and a return to better health. When someone is dying, however, the problems that develop may appear similar, but don't respond to treatment as convincingly. Alternatively, the treatments themselves may appear to cause even more problems. Often it seems that as soon as one problem is fixed, another one appears. In this situation, the problems are actually a sign of a bigger underlying issue, rather than the cause.

That is, when someone is dying we recognise the problems without necessarily recognising the fact they are dying. At this time, treatments previously considered beneficial become futile at the very least; worse still, they may result in greater burden on the dying person. The issue of recognising this medical futility is one of the most challenging aspects of caring for someone with a life-limiting illness.

What to expect in the dying phase

The dying process is unique to each person but in most cases, there are common characteristics or changes that indicate that a person is dying.

Much of the fear surrounding dying is caused by either not knowing what to expect or a concern about specific symptoms or changes. In the following pages, various symptoms and signs seen in dying patients will be discussed. This list is not designed to cause alarm but to provide information. It is very rare for a single person to experience all these problems. People may only have a few of these changes.

At times, problems can be treated in a way that removes the symptoms or at least reduces them to a level that can be tolerated. Treating the problem does not stop the dying process but makes it more tolerable. Some of the following problems, however, may not be specifically treatable, but occur as part of the normal and unavoidable process of dying. Sometimes nothing specific can be done for certain changes other than to acknowledge them, and the dying process, as a normal part of life. Recognising and understanding these changes as part of a normal process can be reassuring at what is often a sad and challenging time for both the dying person and the people close to him or her.

The dying person may need to talk about issues that are important to him or her once he or she knows that he or she is dying, and providing this opportunity is an effective treatment in itself. Most people know if the truth is being kept from them and this tends to cause more anxiety. It is better not to hide reality from a dying person, even though this is often an instinctive way we try to protect others from fear or worry.

Even when someone may only have a few hours to live, it is important they are given time to express fears or wishes to those caring for them. It is often difficult to sit with someone who is dying but for the dying person it is very important to be included in discussions with others, even if it is not about his or her own problems. Sometimes the person may wish to say something important to a friend or relative before he or she becomes too weak to communicate and this time must be provided. When someone is dying, it is important not to use up too much of his or her time with medical interventions, and treatments should be as non-invasive as possible.

The difference between symptoms and signs

Symptoms and signs are very different things. A symptom is something felt by the person with the problem; it is his or her own experience or feeling. A sign is what other people see or find on examination.

A person with a symptom may not have any outward signs, so his or her description helps others to work out what is happening. Examples of symptoms are pain, nausea, and fatigue. Signs of a problem may be present without the person feeling anything is wrong. Examples of signs include a rapid heart rate, high (or low) blood pressure and laboured breathing.

When assessing someone who is sick, health professionals listen to a person's symptoms and examine him or her for signs. From the information gathered and then interpreted, they work out the likely diagnosis and then consider if any tests are required to confirm this. Treatment is then determined based on the diagnosis and the person's needs.

When someone is dying, it may not be appropriate or even necessary to perform investigations before starting treatment. Likewise, certain treatments may be unnecessary. In many cases, treatment provided in the dying phase aims to take away symptoms, even if the cause can't be taken away. Sometimes there may be signs of a problem but the dying person does not feel any symptoms. At these times, there can be a feeling from health professionals or relatives that something must be done for the sign, but this may not help the dying person. Treating a sign may only burden the dying person with more drugs or interventions. At best, the people giving the treatment may feel they have at least tried to do something but, at worst, the treatment may cause its own problems such as an adverse drug reaction or interference with other treatment. In other words, unnecessary treatment may actually cause harm.

Common symptoms and signs

The examples of symptoms and signs below are far from exhaustive. They are given to illustrate a concept; in reality, there are hundreds (maybe thousands) of symptoms and signs. It is important to realise that any one of these signs or symptoms can also occur when people are not dying, but the focus of the following descriptions is on those whose illness has reached a stage so advanced that survival is unlikely. For the rest of this chapter the discussion will focus mainly on people in the last days to hours of life.

Weakness

Weakness affects almost every person with a life-limiting illness, and usually becomes more severe closer to death. It usually refers to the state of decreased strength that makes it more difficult to perform normal tasks. It is due to loss of muscle bulk and power brought on by the continuous demands of the underlying disease on the entire body, which slowly consumes its energy reserves even if the person is trying to conserve them. Sometimes muscle weakness occurs because the nerves that make them work are damaged by the underlying disease. It is both a symptom and a sign.

Weakness is often one of the worst symptoms experienced by a dying person, as it causes so many restrictions on a person's ability to be independent and may leave them feeling helpless. In the early phases of an illness, the change can be subtle to the observer but very distressing to the person as they can't do things that were easy in the past.

As death approaches and different organ systems fail, weakness can be due to many things including the build-up of waste products not being effectively removed by the liver and kidneys, but rather staying in the body and interfering with the normal functioning of muscles and other systems. In addition, the heart may not be able to maintain a strong circulation to deliver oxygen and nutrients to the muscles.

When a person is dying, weakness may be so severe that he or she cannot walk safely or easily due to weakness in the legs. Other signs of severe weakness may be an inability to hold cups or even keep one's eyes open and talk to people. Nearly all people who are dying become bed bound in the last days of life and rely on others to help with their care. With severe weakness even the simplest task such as swallowing fluids and medications or turning in bed becomes impossible.

Possible treatment –
- Occasional turns in bed can help reduce discomfort caused by lying in one position.
- Inserting a urinary catheter into the bladder can remove the need to move a person on and off bed pans to go to the toilet or change the bed linen, which is required if the bed is wet.
- There are no drugs that safely increase muscle strength in people who are dying. Doctors are often asked about anabolic steroids, but these really only work in healthy people and would not reverse the processes that cause weakness.
- In people who are sick but not dying, weakness can be a sign of anaemia and in these people a blood transfusion may help. When someone is dying, blood transfusions don't help even if the person has anaemia.

Fatigue

Fatigue is closely related to weakness and is just as distressing to most people. It is the loss of stamina or ability to complete tasks and is common when muscle weakness is present. It too is the result of the underlying disease using up the person's energy reserves, including their own natural "stress hormones", which usually help them through day-to-day living. A person with severe fatigue may no longer be able even to contemplate starting tasks let alone finish them. It can be confused with lack of motivation or "giving up" but is very different as the sufferer may very much want to do the things that are now impossible.

In the early stages of incurable disease, fatigue may be recognised as an inability to complete all the normal tasks of a healthy day such as working or going out to social events after a busy day. In the dying phase, the person with fatigue may not be able to stay awake for prolonged periods but may need frequent, or sometimes constant, rest. Visitors or family members may feel they are being ignored or snubbed by the person with extreme fatigue, but this is rarely the case.

At this time active treatments and investigations such as blood tests and x-rays can cause distress when the person may prefer to be left alone. A person with physical fatigue may still be mentally strong and alert but just not able to communicate as much. At these times, it is important to include the dying person in discussions even if they don't respond; they may still hear and understand everything that is happening. A person who can understand but not respond can become distressed if others only talk about them and not to them.

Possible treatment –
- Helping the person to minimise exertion.
- Providing an environment that is peaceful and stress free.
- There are no specific drug treatments to reverse fatigue.

Shortness of breath, laboured breathing and altered breathing patterns

Shortness of breath or breathlessness is called dyspnoea (pronounced "disp-near") by medical professionals and means an abnormal awareness of one's own breathing. Although most people think of this as meaning a lack of oxygen, it has many different causes. Some people with dyspnoea might have low oxygen levels but, for many, the levels of oxygen can be normal. On the other hand, someone may have low oxygen levels but not feel breathless. Dyspnoea is a symptom; low oxygen is a sign. Other signs to consider at this time are laboured breathing and other altered breathing patterns.

Dyspnoea can be caused by weakness, a narrowing of the airways by cancer, damage to normal lung tissue, or the collapse of part of the lungs, as seen when an airway becomes totally blocked or the lung is squashed by fluid building up around the lung. Dyspnoea can be very distressing and cause anxiety to the point of panic. When it is less severe, it still restricts how much a person can do independently, and is often brought on by activity. When someone is extremely weak it can occur at rest. Breathlessness may occur when people are dying but as energy demands reduce when they are less active, people may actually find their breathing is easier.

Laboured breathing is an observation made by others when it appears someone is making a greater than normal effort to breathe. It can be apparent even if the person does not feel breathless. It can occur when someone is not yet dying but develops an acute problem such as a pulmonary embolus or chest infection. It is very common when someone is dying. It has many causes similar to dyspnoea but is also seen as death approaches because the brain starts sending a different signal to the lungs, which changes how fast and deep a person breathes.

Other altered breathing patterns may be seen when someone is close to death. As the body has less use for oxygen, the signals that come from the brain to make us breathe become less intense and this is often seen as shallow breathing. This sign may not cause any distressing symptoms. Breathing can become very irregular in terms of rate and depth. Sometimes laboured breathing alternates with pauses in breathing (called Cheyne-Stokes breathing) and may be a sign that death is only hours away. The pauses can last more than 30 seconds and may lead those with the person to think that the person has actually died.

Possible treatment –

- If someone is breathless because of low oxygen, oxygen can be offered. This can be given at a low rate using small plastic tubes resting in the nostrils or at higher rates through a mask. Dying people often find a mask very restricting and if they are still able to talk, it can make communication more difficult. Nasal tubes are often sufficient. Oxygen can be very drying, which can worsen other problems such as dry mouth or thickened secretions and so should only be used if it provides help. As low oxygen levels can sometimes add to delirium (see below), it is also reasonable to use oxygen in this setting even if the person does not feel breathless.

- Minimising unnecessary activity reduces the physical demands that can cause dyspnoea.
- Maintaining a calm environment is very important especially if there is any anxiety associated with breathlessness.
- Fresh air can be a simple and very effective way to provide relief. If the weather is fine and warm, an open window may be enough. Alternatively, a fan can help by moving air and it is understood that the movement of air across the face can be very soothing.
- In some situations, medications can be effective at reducing breathlessness. Treatments usually used for chronic lung conditions like asthma sometimes help, for example salbutamol (Ventolin, Airomir, Asmasal) or ipratropium (Atrovent). There is a fear that certain drugs used in palliative care can hasten death by stopping breathing but this is very unlikely if the right doses are chosen. Some of these drugs can actually provide very good control of symptoms such as dyspnoea without causing any harm. In general, only small doses of these drugs are required to help. Inappropriately large doses don't help any better but may actually be harmful. Careful use of drugs used for anxiety can decrease the distress that comes with breathless episodes. Common examples of these drugs are the family of benzodiazepines such as diazepam (Valium, Tensium), alprazolam (Xanax) and lorazepam (Ativan). In some cases, morphine is very good at reducing breathlessness.

Chest secretions

When weakness becomes severe, it is possible for normal secretions such as saliva and mucous to build up in the throat and chest. Normally these secretions are coughed clear, almost subconsciously, but in the dying phase, this ability is lost. In this situation, a noisy rattle is heard as the person breathes in and out. This is also known as the death rattle and is mostly seen after someone becomes unconscious. It is a good indicator that death may only be a few hours away. It is another example of a sign of dying rather than a symptom. Whilst it is often a distressing sound to listen to, the dying person may not feel any distress. People who are still conscious can be aware of the sound without feeling breathless or wanting anything done about it. Treatment of this sign should only be given if it is causing distressing symptoms.

Possible treatment –

- Changing a person's position may reduce the noise.
- There are drugs available that reduce or dry up the secretions. The main reasons these drugs should not be used if there is no distress is because they add to the person's medication load and they can make breathing more difficult by thickening the secretions through their drying mechanism.

Anxiety and fear

Anxiety is a common symptom with several possible causes including physical, emotional, psychological and spiritual factors. Many of the symptoms and signs described in this chapter can cause it. It can also make other symptoms worse or more difficult to treat, especially when it is not recognised or properly addressed. Other words used to describe anxiety include distress, unhappiness, fear, emotional pain, disquiet or worry. Anxiety is also a sign observed by others, and treatment should be considered whether or not the person reports it. It can occur at any stage of illness but is very common in the dying phase. It can be very difficult to separate this problem from delirium, which is a different situation with different treatments. Sometimes the word agitation is used for either condition, which can make assessment and adequate treatment confusing and difficult.

Possible treatment –

- Specific treatment of the underlying cause may reduce anxiety significantly and it is important to be sure that sedating drugs are not used without attempting to address and control the underlying problem. An example of this is the person who can't empty his or her bladder despite a strong, continuous urge, but then has a catheter inserted, which relieves the pressure and reduces distress and anxiety.
- Minimising stress and anxiety in the person by providing a calm and peaceful environment. When death is approaching, it is very reassuring to know that important people are close by, particularly if the dying person is in an unfamiliar place such as hospital. Sometimes it is relaxing for the dying person to have familiar things around them. A favourite artist or piece of music can provide enjoyment at what can be a very difficult time.

Some people like pleasant scents or smells and aromatherapy can be very useful in this regard.

- Of the medications that can settle anxiety, the most commonly used group are sedatives called benzodiazepines, which are also used to help sleep. Common examples of these are listed on p.34 in the treatment of breathlessness. When used at the right time and in appropriate doses, these drugs can provide great relief without necessarily causing excessive sedation.

Delirium

Delirium is a physical disturbance of brain function, which can cause many symptoms and signs. Unlike the other problems discussed in this chapter it is not so much a symptom or a sign but rather a whole medical diagnosis in itself. A person with delirium shows many signs usually connected to psychiatric illnesses, but in itself it is a medical rather than a psychological or emotional problem. Signs include poor attention, memory loss, paranoid behaviour, disorientation, loss of normal sleep patterns and loss of interest in usual activities. The level of consciousness can be anywhere from very drowsy to overactive and out of proportion to the person's overall poor health. The person may experience hallucinations. It is important for relatives and friends to know that if a delirious person does not recognise them or is aggressive, this is not anybody's fault, and it is not something the dying person can control.

The most typical form of delirium described in medical texts is called psychomotor agitation where the person shows repetitive and confused behaviour, pulling off clothes, constantly trying to move or climb out of bed without clear reason and showing strength far greater than would be expected. This condition is quite different from that of anxiety discussed above and may even be made worse if drugs used for that condition are given alone. For that reason, the use of the word "agitation" may be better not used when caring for a person who is dying; it is better to specify if the person is "anxious" or "delirious".

Delirium is a very common problem in life-limiting illnesses and occurs in most people at some stage of the illness. When someone is not dying, the cause should be actively sought and treated, as many people recover well. However, at least eight out of ten people develop delirium in the last few days of life. In the dying phase, it is often not reversible but it can be controlled with a combination of drug and non-drug measures. There are many possible causes such as multiple organ failure with a build-up of toxins and waste products, loss of normal circulation through the brain, dehydration, urinary retention and infection. In the dying phase, several causes may occur at once. An often overlooked cause is withdrawal from nicotine or alcohol in people who have used these for a long time. If someone is in nicotine withdrawal then a nicotine patch may be more helpful than any other drug. A lack of oxygen is another cause of delirium, which can be easily treated by administering oxygen.

Possible treatment –

- Providing a peaceful and safe environment with familiar items and voices. Avoiding confronting language, repetitive questions and excessive noise.
- Ceasing unnecessary drugs. In the dying phase, it may not be possible to treat the underlying cause and often it is not possible to fully reverse the delirium.
- The best drugs for controlling the problems caused by delirium are known as tranquilisers and are used at other times to treat psychiatric conditions with similar signs and symptoms such as hallucinations and paranoia. When a dying person is distressed by their delirium, it may be appropriate to use sedating drugs in combination with tranquilisers and this is commonly seen in care of the dying. The most commonly used tranquiliser is haloperidol (Serenace). As with other problems in this chapter, it should be possible to use a dose sufficient to help delirium without causing over-sedation. Sometimes when delirium is controlled, the person is then able to relax and catch up on lost sleep and this may be confused with a drug-induced sleep. It must be remembered that, as a normal part of dying, people become less conscious regardless of drugs given.

Feeling sick (nausea) and vomiting

Nausea is a symptom in which the person feels as if he or she may vomit. Nausea can occur without vomiting, but it is uncommon to have vomiting without nausea. There are many causes for nausea and vomiting in life-limiting illnesses, and these problems frequently occur in dying patients. It is commonly a distressing symptom, both for the patient and his or her family and friends, and is therefore actively treated. If there is a simple cause for nausea, this should be treated, but usually the cause is not simple. In conditions like cancer there can be a combination of physical problems within the gut and chemical disturbances that stimulate areas in the brain, which then trigger vomiting in a reflex action. Nausea and vomiting can be made worse by other uncontrolled symptoms such as pain.

Possible treatment –

- There are many different drugs that treat nausea and these work in different areas within the gut and brain. Commonly used drugs include metoclopramide (Maxalon), cyclizine (Valoid), levomepromazine (Nozinan) and haloperidol, which is also used to treat delirium as above. Due to the multiple possible causes of nausea, it is often necessary to use multiple drugs. These can usually be given as injections to ensure the drug enters the body and gets to work rather than administering tablets that may simply be vomited up again. If distress is present, it may also be necessary to use some sedation, but many drugs used for nausea are also mildly sedating.

Anorexia

Anorexia is a loss of desire to eat, or a lack of hunger or appetite. When a person develops a life-limiting illness, it is very common for appetite to become poor. Anorexia is also common in illnesses that are not life threatening such as the common cold. It is caused by the disease itself and is made worse by problems such as nausea, weakness, fatigue and pain.

From the time we are born we are encouraged and even forced to eat and drink, and there is always concern if someone runs out of food or can't eat for any reason. There is a strong feeling that if someone doesn't eat they will get sick. Sometimes people have no desire to eat any food even when they feel they should. It is a problem often reported by family members, fearing the person will get sicker if they don't eat. Mostly, however, the reality is that the person can't eat because they are sick. If someone forces themselves to eat, they can make nausea worse.

When someone is having difficulty eating through decreased appetite, it is advisable that he or she eats whatever he or she wishes even if it doesn't conform to "normal" dietary rules. Sometimes people only want sweet things, other times only a single food item. Reducing the serving size can be helpful, as the sight of a full plate can cause further loss of hunger. Having more frequent but smaller meals sometimes helps increase the amount of food taken over the whole day. If someone is not eating just because weakness makes it physically difficult, then providing help will be appreciated.

Anorexia is even more dramatic in the dying phase. It is rare for a dying person to feel hungry or thirsty. A rapid decrease in appetite may be a sign that someone is dying. It can also be a way the body protects itself from further harm from issues such as poor swallow and an inability to absorb and metabolise food when the intestine, liver and even kidneys begin to fail.

Although it is a common cause of concern for the person and especially his or her carers, it is not essential for a dying person to eat or drink. It is a natural response to provide nourishment to loved ones, and it is distressing if they will not eat. Relatives may feel offended if the dying person does not want to eat the food they've prepared but this is not anybody's fault. The dying person may even become distressed if they feel they are letting others down by not eating, so it is important to recognise that eating is not as important as other issues in the dying phase. Death will not be accelerated because a person does not eat.

This is far different from a healthy person not eating or being denied access to food. Death is not happening because the person is not eating; the person is not eating because they are dying. At this time, it is still important to provide care and attention, but when feeding is not desired or possible, other things can be equally appreciated such as spending time talking about shared memories or giving news on family and friends. When someone is dying, measures such as steroids do not usually work and it is more important to accept this as part of the process of dying.

Possible treatment –

- At earlier phases of a severe illness, people are often given a course of medication called corticosteroids (steroids, for short) to try to stimulate appetite. Commonly used steroids include prednisolone and dexamethasone. Steroids are actually anti-inflammatory drugs used in conditions like asthma and arthritis, but a common side effect is to cause increased appetite. They have many long-term side effects, so even if they successfully increase appetite, they are usually not used forever.
- Later on, the person should eat whatever they wish, irrespective of whether this conforms to normal dietary rules.
- Eating little and often can increase overall food intake.

Weight loss

Weight loss is very common in many severe illnesses and is not simply due to a drop in food intake. Even when diet is normal, people with advanced disease lose weight and in itself this is usually a strong sign that their condition is deteriorating. Most dying people have already lost a lot of weight and are very thin, with loss of muscle mass and fat stores. This uncontrolled loss of weight is due to a process called cachexia, which is a complex problem that affects nearly every organ and body system and causes exhaustion of all the body's reserves. It can be caused by the disease itself as well as the body's own attempts to fight the disease. Weight loss is the most common sign of cachexia and this process can develop over many weeks or even months before it becomes obvious.

In most people with life-limiting illness, cachexia is a major underlying cause of deterioration and death. It cannot be reversed or even slowed by eating more or using artificial feeding.

Possible treatment –

- Although there may be treatments for this problem in the future, there are no convincing ones at present. So in these circumstances, there is nothing that can reverse cachexia and the weight loss it causes.

Poor swallowing

The development of poor swallowing usually results from progressive generalised weakness and a decrease in the level of consciousness. This means the person loses the ability to eat and drink easily. There is also a risk that things can accidentally go down into the lungs and add to problems like breathlessness and coughing. In the earlier phases of life-limiting illnesses, some patients develop swallowing problems because of issues such as physical blockage by a tumour or damage to nerves that control swallowing. At these times, aggressive interventions are used to help maintain intake of food and fluid, especially if the person is otherwise well.

During the dying phase, all patients lose the ability to swallow at some stage. In addition to food and drink, the dying person becomes unable to swallow medications safely, which affects his or her ability to take medications important for controlling other symptoms such as pain, nausea, delirium and distress. The main aspects of managing poor swallowing in the dying phase are to recognise this as another normal sign, to stop unnecessary medications and to change the way important medications are given. This usually means giving medications by injection; a few medications can be given in other ways such as skin patches, inhalers and nebulisers, and occasionally rectally. This will be discussed later in the chapter.

The dying process will not be influenced by the person's ability to eat or drink. When a person's swallow has failed, it is therefore not essential to try to feed him or her and it may even cause more problems, such as breathlessness and coughing, if things go into the lungs accidentally. Should a person still be awake enough to request something to eat or drink, often just a small taste of a favourite food item or drink is enough to provide satisfaction.

Possible treatment –
- There are no specific drugs that can make swallowing stronger or safer.

Dry or sore mouth

There are many causes of a dry or sore mouth when people are dying and these two symptoms often occur together. Sometimes, swallowing difficulties are made worse by these symptoms. A dry or sore mouth can occur due to drugs, continuous oxygen or increased effort of breathing. Dehydration may also cause a dry mouth. At other times, advanced illness weakens the immune system, which allows the development of a fungal infection in the mouth, called thrush, and this can also cause these symptoms.

Possible treatment –
- General mouth care, including regular moistening and cleaning of the mouth and tongue.
- When a person is too drowsy or weak, then help can be given by others using moistened swabs or sprays.
- Thrush can be treated with specially targeted antifungal medications, some of which can be placed directly into the mouth as drops.

Decreased fluid intake and dehydration

Most people drink less fluid in the days before death. Decreased fluid intake is due to a combination of progressive weakness, which makes the act of drinking more difficult, along with the loss of thirst and desire to drink, which is a normal part of the dying process. Dehydration is a sign that indicates the body lacks the normal level of fluid. It can develop slowly when a person has decreased intake of food and fluids due to anorexia but can come on very quickly with other problems such as vomiting. Dehydration does not usually cause distress to the dying person.

Possible treatment –

- Good mouth care should be given.
- It is totally reasonable to offer fluids orally. If the patient cannot swallow safely, then good mouth care, keeping the mouth and tongue moist, often alleviates the sensation of dry mouth and thirst.
- If someone is thirsty, oral measures and occasionally artificial fluids given through a needle under the skin may alleviate their symptoms. Usually, artificial fluids are not given to dying people, but this decision is made on the needs of the individual.

Muscle twitches, spasms and seizures

Occasionally people develop involuntary movements in their muscles in the dying phase. These movements can be occasional twitches of small muscles in the hands or face but, in more severe forms, spasms can cause marked jerking of the limbs. This is often a sign that does not cause distress but can be alarming to see. If someone is still conscious, these movements can interfere with actions that require steadiness such as holding a cup for a drink. Such involuntary movements can be caused by a build-up of waste products including medication by-products particularly when the kidneys or liver start failing. Other problems such as delirium may occur at the same time. Sometimes extremely weak and fatigued muscles develop a tremor, which can appear similar.

Possible treatment –

- Often no specific treatment is needed for this sign, and it may be that reducing unnecessary drugs can reduce the toxic load on the body.
- If twitches and jerks cause distress, some drugs can reduce these events, particularly those used at other times in life to stop epileptic fits. A commonly used anticonvulsant drug is clonazepam (Rivotril), which is also a benzodiazepine, meaning it has sedating properties. Convulsions or seizures are rare in the dying phase but may occur in people with brain tumours or head injuries. The same drugs can treat and even prevent these from occurring.

Failure of circulation

As death approaches, various organ systems start to shut down, including the circulation of blood. The body prioritises blood flow in the last days and hours of life to the brain, heart and lungs. Common signs of failure of circulation at these times are due to the loss of blood supply to the skin, which can become pale or mottled in appearance, and moist or cool to touch. Swelling may develop in the hands and feet, as fluid is not returned as easily to the heart. These signs do not usually cause any symptoms and by this stage people are often drowsy and even unconscious.

Possible treatment –
- No specific treatment is needed for this sign, and its development usually means death is only hours away.

Withdrawing from the world

As death becomes closer, people spend more time asleep than awake. When awake they may appear drowsier and less interested in their surroundings. Whilst of concern to family and friends, this lack of interest is not a deliberate ignoring of others nor is it a sign of depression. This natural process of withdrawing from the world may actually be accompanied by feelings of tranquillity and acceptance by the dying person. People who have been greatly troubled by symptoms like pain can rapidly become comfortable and free from distress in the last days to hours of life. A sudden decrease in distress is a strong sign that death may only be hours away. At these times, other signs described earlier develop, such as altered breathing patterns, noisy secretions and cool skin.

withdrawing from the world may actually be accompanied by feelings of tranquillity and acceptance by the dying person.

When a dying person appears asleep and unrousable, it is not certain if they are aware of their surroundings. Sometimes people appear to respond to familiar voices and this appears to be a comforting experience. At these times, it is not known if they understand specific words, but people are able to spend what may be their last opportunity talking to a close friend or relative before they die. This can be a very important time for the dying person as well as those they are leaving.

Possible treatment –
- No specific treatment is required, as death is imminent.

Pain

Pain is probably the symptom most feared when people think about dying from an incurable illness. It is not just a physical symptom caused by damage to part of the body but rather an entire, unpleasant experience influenced by emotional, personal and environmental factors. Pain is caused by many things depending on the underlying disease and is a very individual symptom. No two people have identical pain, meaning the assessment and treatment of pain is different for every person and even for different episodes within the same person. Sometimes pain can be terrible, even when there is little to find on physical examination or investigations such as x-rays. Other symptoms and problems can worsen pain, even if they don't cause it. Depending on its cause and other issues, pain will not go away if the only strategy used is pain-relieving drugs.

Although feared, pain does not just occur simply because someone is dying and not every dying person will experience pain. If someone has not had pain during their life-limiting illness, it is probable they will not experience severe pain in their final days. Likewise, if someone has had stable pain control for many weeks or months, there is no reason for it to suddenly change just because they are dying. Pain can get worse, however, if the underlying cause is getting worse, as seen when an invasive cancer continues to grow.

For many dying patients other problems cause more distress and limitations to their life, even when pain is severe. At times people express pain as a symptom when in fact several distressing feelings are occurring together. For example, extreme fatigue and weakness can cause an all-over feeling of pain, which does not get better even if significant doses of pain relief are given. People with distress or delirium can feel marked discomfort without a definite focus or cause of increased pain. Again, pain-relieving drugs may not help these people. Pain will be best treated when a thorough understanding of that person's pain is gained to allow the best targeting of the problem.

At times, simple non-drug therapies provide good pain relief. For someone too weak to move freely, occasional turns in bed can relieve pressure-related pain successfully. Providing gentle stimulation to other senses may also help reduce the sensation of pain; gentle massage, music and aromatherapy can be very useful in this regard. If the urinary bladder is full and can't empty easily, a urinary catheter can be very relieving. Similarly, if someone has not used their bowels for several days, an enema or suppository may reduce discomfort by helping the bowels to open. For issues like fear and anxiety, providing time, listening and talking can be the most effective treatment. In many situations, however, there is a definite need for pain-relieving drugs. Well over half of all people with cancer do experience pain during their illness and providing adequate pain relief is a major priority in the care of the dying.

Pain relief

It is not the aim of this book to provide an encyclopaedic reference to all drug treatments for pain. Sometimes there are several options for pain relief, and in many cases they are very helpful. The exact drugs chosen depend on such factors as the person's need, local availability of drugs, the safety of various drugs and how the person can actually take them. When symptoms become worse, drug doses need to be reviewed and sometimes new drugs started or added to existing ones. Depending on the person's problem it may be necessary to change the way the drug is given.

The strength of a drug used depends on the severity of the pain and how well the person responds to the drug. The box on p.46 lists commonly used pain relievers with some of their brand names. This list does not represent every available drug but is just a sample.

When pain is mild, then a mild drug such as paracetamol should be sufficient. With more severe pain, stronger drugs are needed. One such class are anti-inflammatory drugs, which are used to treat muscular and joint problems such as arthritis and include ibuprofen, diclofenac, piroxicam and celecoxib.

The most commonly used pain relievers are called opioids, derived from the poppy plant, which has been used for centuries to make opium. For mild to moderate pain, weak opioids may be sufficient. The most common weak opioid is codeine, which is present in many supermarket and pharmacy pain relievers. It is often combined with paracetamol and sold as co-codamol. A newer drug closely related to opioids is tramadol.

For more severe pain, the most commonly prescribed drugs are the strong opioids such as morphine. There are many people who feel uncomfortable at the idea of being given morphine. Inappropriate use of these drugs such as recreational drug abuse, medical negligence or deliberate misuse, and international political conflicts (for example, the opium wars) has resulted in many people worldwide being reluctant to use them. In certain countries, some or all of these drugs are not available or highly restricted. When used at the right time and in the right doses, these drugs are not addictive and are safe. Contrary to what many people believe, they should not directly accelerate death when used appropriately. To decrease the risk of unnecessary death, only the minimum dose required to help a problem should be used.

If a drug does not work unless it is given in a large enough dose to render someone unconscious or kill them, it is probably because it was not the right drug to help that person's problem. It is important to recognise that when someone is dying, the process continues whether or not drugs are given. It is unfortunate that people still die with poorly controlled pain because there is a mistaken belief that dying could be slowed or avoided by not using pain-relieving drugs.

Commonly used drugs for pain relief

Drug strength	Drug name	Alternative or brand names
Mild	paracetamol	acetaminophen, Panadol
	aspirin	Alka-Seltzer, Aspro Clear, Disprin,
Anti-inflammatory	ibuprofen	Brufen, Advil, Nurofen
	diclofenac	Voltarol, Motifene, Arthrotec
	piroxicam	Feldene
	celecoxib	Celebrex
Weak opioids	codeine	
	tramadol	Zydol, Dromadol
Combinations	paracetamol/codeine	co-codamol, Panadeine, Kapake, Tylex
	paracetamol/tramadol	Tramacet
Strong opioids	morphine	Oramorph, Sevredol, MST, MXL
	diamorphine	Heroin
	hydromorphone	Palladone
	oxycodone	OxyNorm, OxyContin
	fentanyl	Durogesic
	methadone	Physeptone

How should the drug be taken? When someone is able to swallow safely, the most appropriate way to take pain-relieving drugs is by mouth using tablets, capsules or liquids. If pain is an ongoing problem, then it is best to give drugs regularly to avoid letting pain build up and going out of control. When there is a loss of pain control, then often larger doses are required to regain control, and this carries the risk of increased side effects. Many of the strong opioids now have slow-release preparations that only need to be taken once or twice a day, and fentanyl is made in a skin patch that only needs to be changed every three days.

What happens if more pain occurs? As conditions like cancer progress, the symptoms can change and sometimes get worse. Even when someone is taking their medications as directed, pain can still happen and these episodes are sometimes referred to as "breakthrough pain" meaning the pain breaks through the protection the drugs are aiming to provide. This is a well-recognised problem and for that reason most people are provided with back-up supplies of medication for these episodes. This usually consists of a medication they are already taking but given in a short-acting form in an amount much smaller than the total daily dose.

If someone is consistently requiring extra doses of pain relief every day, then a total review of their symptoms is required and either the dose of regular pain relief is increased or a new drug is tried. Sometimes this means swapping an old drug for a new one, whilst at other times the new drug is added on top of the others already being taken. When these usually successful approaches do not work it may be necessary for pain specialists, who are specially trained anaesthetists, to be consulted. They can perform more invasive treatments such as local anaesthetic injections, nerve blocks and epidurals.

Giving medicine to the dying person

When someone is dying, it is important that any medication is administered in a sympathetic way. As the person becomes weaker, it is necessary to tailor dosage and method of administration to his or her changing requirements.

What if someone can no longer swallow tablets or liquids?

When someone is dying, it often becomes impossible to give drugs by mouth. At this time, it is common to give drugs by injection. The most common injection is one given just under the skin, called a subcutaneous injection. It is very uncommon, and usually unnecessary, to give injections deep into muscle or into veins via a drip line. Drugs given under the skin can either be given as separate injections or as a continuous infusion delivered by one of several types of machine usually called a syringe driver (*see below*).

Are injections only given when someone is dying?

There are other situations where injections may be required. They are commonly required when someone has frequent vomiting and can't absorb tablets or liquids well. Some drugs do not exist in an oral form and can only be effective when injected. In addition, there may be a need for a drug to work quickly, in which case injections are usually better than tablets.

What is a syringe driver?

Syringe drivers are machines purpose built to provide the controlled delivery of drugs, and are frequently used to maintain symptom control in dying patients. Many people need to commence syringe drivers when they can no longer swallow drugs they have been using for controlling pain and other symptoms. The most commonly used syringe drivers are battery-powered and only need to be filled once a day. For people in their own homes, a community nurse visits to prepare and set up the syringe driver. They are also used in hospital. The drugs required are calculated and prescribed by a doctor after discussion with the patient and the nurse. Once available, they are drawn up into a syringe. A needle is placed under the skin and a short plastic tube joins this to the syringe. The syringe is then put into the machine, which is programmed to push the medication in slowly over the whole day.

It is usually possible to put many drugs into the one syringe to help control pain, nausea, anxiety and other symptoms. The doses can be reviewed every day to make sure enough is being provided. If a symptom is not well enough controlled, then the syringe can be changed and a higher dose of drug given. Also, it is easy to decrease the amount if it is felt to be too strong, or change the combination if needed. These machines are safe to use and often family members are taught how to keep an eye on them between nursing visits to be sure the batteries don't go flat and the machine keeps working.

Syringe drivers are sometimes used when a person is not dying for very similar reasons as discussed above for injections. The most common reason is when someone develops vomiting and cannot take their medications by mouth. There can be anxiety when a syringe driver is started in these situations because it may be misinterpreted that the person must be dying. Once the vomiting stops, most people stop using the syringe driver and return to using tablets.

Syringe drivers are sometimes used when a person is not dying …

Also, there is sometimes a mistaken belief that drugs are being infused through a driver at doses designed to deliberately hasten death, and this can cause distress amongst relatives who think death is happening because the driver is starting. Like many situations earlier in this chapter, it needs to be explained that the person is being started on the driver because they are dying and still need to have their symptoms controlled; they are not dying because of the driver.

What if the syringe driver does not control the symptoms? If the amount of medication in the syringe driver is not enough, people are usually provided with access to extra doses to inject when required. This is done in the same way as described earlier for pain relief but can also work for other symptoms such as nausea and anxiety. It is not unusual for a dying person to have a range of drugs available for use as required. There are many names for these doses including "top-up", "breakthrough", "rescue" or "prn". The daily calculation of the syringe driver dose takes into account how much drug was in the syringe driver as well as the extra doses required to keep the person comfortable.

Can medication be harmful? There is a belief in some quarters that a dying person's death will be caused or at least hastened by the effects of the drugs used to control symptoms.

At times, phrases such as "slow euthanasia" or "euthanasia by stealth" get used when people talk about palliative care, particularly with respect to the use of syringe drivers and powerful medications. It is important to consider the differences between having a good death with the help of palliative care and the act of euthanasia.

When someone is dying, good palliative care aims to provide comfort to that person by making the process as free of distress as possible. In many situations, drugs are required to provide symptom control to alleviate distress, as has been discussed throughout this chapter. When used at the right time and at the right doses, they will not hasten death. This is very different from the deliberate act of euthanasia, where a person requests to die. With euthanasia, the drugs used and the doses given are deliberately calculated to make the person stop breathing and to stop their heart, before their body is ready to die.

One of the principal arguments used by advocates of euthanasia is that diseases like incurable cancer cause uncontrollable symptoms, and loss of dignity, and that people should not have to die with these symptoms. The very word "euthanasia" is derived from ancient Greek meaning "a good death" and the inference made by pro-euthanasia advocates is that this is the only way one can ensure a good death. This inference is not true; most people experience a good death by allowing nature to take its course.

… *"euthanasia"* is derived from ancient Greek meaning *"a good death"* …

The misconception that palliative care and euthanasia are different words for the same process results in some people not seeking or accepting good palliative care due to a fear that their life will be shortened if they receive such care. For those with poorly controlled pain or other symptoms, the process of dying can then become unnecessarily distressing. It is unfortunate to think that misconceptions about the aims of palliative care as opposed to euthanasia lead to some people dying in the very situation argued by pro-euthanasia advocates as justification for its legalisation.

When a person has their symptoms assessed and treated appropriately, and at the right time, it is unlikely they will die in unnecessary distress. "Euthanasia" is not required for "a good death".

Stopping drugs

In addition to starting or increasing drugs to control distressing symptoms, an important part of good palliative care is to be sure a person is not taking drugs unnecessarily. Drugs that may have been important in a previous part of life may no longer be necessary but may interact with newer medications and add to the dying person's burden. The timely cessation of drugs is just as important as starting new treatments. It is important, however, not to stop drugs in a way that may cause a problem. Some drugs need to be reduced slowly to avoid withdrawal effects; examples of these drugs are steroids, nicotine, and sleeping pills.

How is all this care managed?

With so many potential problems developing in the dying phase, it is important to have access to health professionals who are confident and experienced in helping people living with a life-limiting illness. Specialist palliative care services exist throughout the country and consist of teams of doctors, nurses, other health professionals and therapists as well as volunteers, all with different skills important in the care of patients with complex needs. These services not only aim to help patients but also their families, as well as other health professionals, including the family GP, who provide care for the person living with the life-limiting illness. Palliative care specialists have training in management of various symptoms and signs that occur in the dying phase and are able to advise and prescribe medications required at these times.

For this care to work effectively, good communication skills are required so that information is shared by all those responsible for the person's care. In many cases, the family GP still carries the responsibility of prescribing the necessary drugs, and good communication is essential between all parties, not only to make sure important drugs are prescribed and adjusted as needed, but also to decrease the chance of adverse drug interactions. In some circumstances, the problems encountered in the dying phase may require minimal specialist intervention, in which case the family with their GP may be able to manage the situation as a team. In more complex situations, regular advice and review from palliative care teams may be required to help manage the situation.

In some circumstances, it is impossible to manage the situation at home and it is not uncommon for people to be admitted to specialist palliative care units, or hospices. Sometimes these admissions allow time for problems to be sorted out to enable the person to return home again. At other times it is recognised that the person is dying and should be cared for in the hospice until he or she dies, as the combination of needs would make it too difficult to successfully provide care at home.

Chapter 2 Communication and coping emotionally

Learning that a loved one is dying is one of the worst things that can happen to us. Sadly, it is inevitable that we will all, at some point in our lives, lose a close relative or friend. We will feel a mass of different emotions, which at times will seem completely jumbled and out of control. Each of us will face this news with a lifetime of personal experiences that will impact on how we feel and behave in this situation.

It is important to emphasise one thing, however obvious it may seem: everyone is different. Although it is impossible to provide a set of hard-and-fast rules on how to communicate, certain things that people say and do really can help those who are dying.

There are no scripts when it comes to dying

First of all it seems right to clarify from the start what this chapter cannot do. There can be no set script that you can use when talking to someone who may be dying. And there are, unfortunately, no deep words of wisdom you can recite that will make everything all right.

Films and television have a lot to answer for. Talking about difficult situations seems so easy. The words just flow. No stuttering, uncomfortable pauses or fumbled sentences. Loved ones say words of comfort eloquently and with ease. Years of feuds and problems are resolved by one heart-rending speech that seamlessly unites a family. It is no surprise really, since those beautiful words have been written by a team of skilled scriptwriters and revised after several rehearsals.

This chapter does not deal with the sort of drama that is seen on television. It concentrates on the realities faced in the real world, when we receive the awful news that someone we care for is dying. Similarly, the quotations are from real patients and their families, many of whom prefer to remain anonymous. In all cases, though, their personal experiences, whilst unique, are easily applied to our lives.

Common reactions to learning that someone is dying

Just as we have many different emotions when we absorb the news that someone is dying, the person who has been told that they are dying may also experience some or all of the following feelings –

- shock
- anger
- denial
- fear
- blame and guilt
- depression
- acceptance
- relief

Absorbing the news that someone is dying

Learning that a loved one is dying has a profound effect on us. Although true and accurate, the previous sentence is a ridiculously matter-of-fact, if not trite, statement. Here is another way of putting it: learning that someone you care for is dying can be devastating. Your whole world falls apart. It is the worst feeling in the world. You feel completely out of control, and experience a barrage of emotions all at the same time and in such a disorganised way that you cannot really identify how you feel about anything. We all react differently to devastating news because we each have our individual personalities and experiences. Your feelings and how you show them will be unique. However, most people have some broadly common experiences. It is worth being aware of them, if only to reassure yourself that your feelings at this awful time are normal for what you are going through.

Shock

When we are first told that someone we care for is dying, it is likely to be a huge shock. People often describe feeling numb, as if it is all unreal. It almost feels as if it isn't really happening. Sometimes you feel so numb that you are unable to express any emotion.

"Everyone said I took the news that my dad was dying really well, that I took it all calmly. In reality I was so shocked that I didn't know what to say or do. I suppose I looked calm because I was too numb to show any reaction."

When we are shocked by bad news, we are unlikely to take on board everything that has been said. People remember only small amounts of information and very few details. This is very normal. This can be difficult if you need to tell other friends or family the news because you may feel you cannot remember all that was said.

When we are shocked by bad news, we are unlikely to take on board everything that has been said.

Do not be afraid to ask questions or clarify what has been said to you. It is normal to need to ask the same questions over and over again.

Anger

Anger is a common emotion to feel. We have felt numb for a while and then the mist seems to lift from our mind and we try to get back to normal brain function again. We feel a massive influx of emotions and sometimes it is all too much to cope with.

We seem to have more questions in our head than answers. Being angry is often an easier option for our brains to cope with, although the focus of our anger can be variable. We may get angry with the doctors:

"Why can't they make Mum better? They're rubbish! They don't know what they're doing."

"I knew something was wrong with her! The GP has a lot to answer for. If he had done his job and diagnosed this sooner she would be fine."

Deep down we know that everything has been done properly but we need to focus our distress somewhere. We put so much faith in the medical profession that when someone we care for does not get better, we feel that someone must be blamed.

The sad rules of life are these:
Rule number one: *people die*
Rule number two: *doctors cannot always prevent rule number one.*

We may get angry with those around us. Family members may come under attack for things that would not normally bother us. We may say things to them that we don't really mean. If this is the case with you, you don't have to feel guilty about your anger or thoughts. The feelings you have are normal. If you are religious, you may feel angry towards your God. Sometimes people have a huge crisis of faith when faced with a loved one's death.

"If God is such a loving God, why did He allow this to happen?"

The author of the Narnia books, C.S. Lewis, was a very devout Christian. When his wife, Joy Davidson, died of cancer, Lewis had huge crises regarding his faith and his relationship with God. He wrote about it in the book *A Grief Observed*, which was made into the film *Shadowlands* starring Anthony Hopkins and Deborah Winger. The book and the film depict powerfully and accurately how we feel when a loved one is dying.

Denial

Some of us cope with bad news by pretending it isn't happening. We deny or choose to disbelieve the news. *"If I don't acknowledge it, it can't be happening."* We carry on as if nothing has changed, putting up barriers to avoid talking about it. We may decide to ask no questions about the situation and to talk about it as little as possible. For some people, this is the only way to cope. It is often helpful to talk these feelings through with someone, although for some people it may be the only way for them to keep things together, so they should never be forced to confront a reality they do not want to face.

Fear

This is a normal feeling. You may have all sorts of reasons to be scared. You may worry about how you will cope with the loved one's death. How will you tell other friends the news? What should you do now?

We tend to fear the unknown because we cannot prepare for it or make plans to cope with it. Sometimes it is not the unknown that causes the fear but rather our previous experiences – the known.

"When I heard that my dad was dying I just went to pieces. I remember my nan being so distressed and dying in pain that I was terrified the same would happen to him as well."

It is important to talk these things through. Often our previous experiences of a loved one's death are very different from what is happening now. Also, care of the dying has progressed immensely over the past few years.

Blame and guilt

Sometimes, in trying to find reasons why someone is dying or why a loved one's illness has happened, we blame ourselves or other people. This is sometimes because we think we will feel better if we can understand why something has happened.

We might blame the doctors for not diagnosing the illness quickly enough or being able to offer a cure.

"I can't believe in this day and age that we can put men on the moon but we can't cure cancer. What are the doctors playing at?"

Sometimes we blame ourselves, thinking that we could have done more. Perhaps we should have made him or her see the doctor sooner. Maybe we should have made him or her stop smoking. There are usually a lot of different factors that come together to make someone so ill that they are dying. Some people may be prone to certain illnesses because of the genes they inherited. Some diseases are associated with lifestyle decisions like smoking or diet. There is rarely one single factor that accounts for an illness, and even less reason to blame yourself or someone else. Nevertheless, it is sometimes hard to get rid of these feelings. Talking them through with someone does help.

Depression

As sad news sinks in, it is not unusual to feel low and get depressed. Often our mind is a whirr of thoughts about what we are going to do and how we will cope. We sleep poorly and become increasingly tired. Our concentration goes and we lose interest in the things we used to enjoy taking part in.

Sometimes our low mood is just an appropriate response to sad news. Talking things through may help. However, it is important to be aware that sometimes we can become seriously depressed during periods of severe stress and sadness. It is important to see your GP if you or others feel that you are becoming low in mood.

Acceptance

Having refused to believe that someone is dying, having got angry with the entire world, we usually get to a point where we finally accept that the bad news we received is true. This acceptance is often accompanied by a sense of peace and calm. People sometimes describe a feeling of clarity when they are once more able to think coherently. Acceptance does not mean you are happy about the news; it just means you have got to a point where you believe what is being said and your mind is able to handle information a little better.

Relief

This is quite a common feeling to have but one we feel guilty admitting to. If we have observed a loved one suffer for a long time with a terminal illness, we may view death as a peaceful release. Sometimes we may have observed a loved one in hospital and thought that he or she appeared to be dying, yet no one else thought so. It is often a relief to be told that that person is near the end and will be kept comfortable.

What someone who is dying needs from you

We have talked about how we might feel when we learn that a loved one is dying. We accept that it will have a huge impact on us emotionally for many reasons. However, it is essential to remember the following:

This is not about us!
It is about the person who is dying.

I know this may sound obvious but sometimes we get so affected by bad news that we forget about the person who is dying.

"What am I going to do? How will I manage?"

"What are they going to say at work if I need time off?"

These questions may sound selfish, but they are completely normal. We all ask them to some degree, we just don't admit it. We get so worried about how we are going to cope and what we need to do to get through this, that the needs of our loved one may get overlooked for a moment, and we get wrapped up in our own needs and concerns. As a result, this can be a lonely time for everyone – for the one who is dying, as well as for those around who have to stand by and watch.

Yet a dying person will have many needs during their illness. He or she will have physical needs such as control of symptoms and "hands on" physical care. He or she may have financial needs, which they want to put in order before they die. Some people will have spiritual or religious needs. The key question is, what do they need from you? Their symptom control needs are likely to be addressed by the health professionals involved in their care and it wouldn't be appropriate for you to start prescribing medicines since you are not trained for this. Likewise, you would ask someone suitably qualified to deal with the financial issues rather than attempt to do so yourself and risk getting things wrong. You shouldn't therefore feel that you must sort out problems that you don't have the skills to deal with, if there is someone better qualified for the job.

One way to approach the question of what the dying person needs from you is to consider what he or she needed from you when they *weren't* dying. If you are the person's partner, that's what he or she still needs: someone to be there. If he or she was your mate who you went down to the pub and talked rubbish with, that's what he or she needs now: someone to hang out with. The person didn't choose you because he or she thought that you had excellent counselling skills that might come in handy should he or she get a terminal illness. He or she chose you because he or she liked you. You were someone to talk to in the good times. Now he or she needs you in the bad times. The person isn't expecting things beyond what you can deliver. He or she just wants someone who reminds him or her of normality.

"I've been on this planet 62 years. I've raised a family, travelled the world and worked in the village shop most of my life. I've had cancer for six months and that's all people see me for. I'm someone with cancer. The cancer doesn't define me. The 61½ years before the cancer define me."

Looked at in a different way, one of the most upsetting things for people who know they are dying is the lack of control. When we are well, we can do pretty much what we please. We can get up when we want, eat what we want, go out when we like and not worry about things too much. A terminal illness removes that control. People who are dying may have gone through long periods of treatment, which have been dictated by their GP and the hospital. Their life may have revolved around appointments that other people have organised for them. They may require help to get out of bed or go to the toilet. A quick walk down to the pub may be a monumental trip. Where is the control in that? The illness has transformed them from a fit, independent person to someone with very little autonomy and control over their lives. It is a very abnormal situation and what they need is normality.

You, however, provide them with one of those "touchstones of normality". You were part of their life before they became ill and you remind them of nice, normal parts of their life.

Remember: the illness does not define them.

Another frustration that people who are dying experience is when others make decisions on their behalf without asking their opinion. This is called paternalism. Although it is often done for the best of motives, it is another way of removing control from the life of someone who already feels unable to influence the world around them. Despite the good intentions, it often has bad consequences.

"We were going to have a family get-together before I became ill, but my daughters cancelled it because they thought it would be too much for me. I know they meant it the right way but I wish someone had asked me. I'm not senile, you know."

From conversations with patients who are dying, it seems that the thing they value most from friends, loved ones and professionals is openness and honesty. Admitting that you don't know what to say is more valued than some banal comment offering false hope or promises you cannot keep. They are not looking for you to make it all right. They just want you to be you. We do not as a rule transform into an "all-singing, all-dancing crisis superbeing" when someone is dying, and the loved one doesn't expect you to be one. They just require you. An open, honest approach that offers availability on their terms is, I believe, the best way. If a loved one feels you are being straight and open with them, you will be the one they turn to if they have specific needs.

Talking to friends and relatives

As if it wasn't enough having to cope with a loved one dying, it may fall to you to tell friends and family the sad news. This is a bit of a double-edged sword. In one sense, it is a privilege that you have been given this important task. You may not have asked for it, but you're doing it. It gives you a certain degree of control that may allow you to protect your loved one from too much. However, it can also be a stressful role. You will be the one getting all the enquiring phone calls and well-wishes. Some people, despite being well-intentioned, will offer unhelpful advice or criticism regarding the care the dying person is getting. Although it isn't meant personally, at this sensitive time you can't help feeling that all negative comments are somehow directed at you.

Before you pass the news on, it is important to prepare for this properly. You have just been given bad news: was it done sensitively and with care? Did the person give you the opportunity to ask questions? Did they explain everything clearly? In essence, if the bad news was broken well, try to take the good points and adapt them when you tell friends and family. Similarly, you may have noticed that the person who broke the news to you arranged to be somewhere you wouldn't be disturbed, and where you had the opportunity to sit down in comfort. The person may have recapped quickly on what has happened, before updating you on how things are now.

In your preparation, make sure you understand what is going on. Have you understood the information that was given to you? You don't need to be familiar with every minor detail, but do make sure you have an understanding of what you are going to say. Think about who you are going to tell. Do you need to tell a whole group in one go or is it better talking to a few people at a time? Are you able to give the news face to face (which is preferable) or can it be done by telephone or even in a letter?

Remember what a shock it was when you were told the news. Make sure you give the information with care and compassion. Each person is different and just because you took the news calmly, it doesn't mean everyone else will. It is possible that you were one of the first to be told because you do handle bad news calmly. Other people may get extremely upset and it is important for you to understand that any such upset or anger is not aimed at you personally; it is simply a sign of distress at the news.

Whenever you give bad news to someone, it is best to prepare them in some way for what news is coming. This is like firing a warning shot of a gun. You may want to start with something like:

"I need to talk to you about Bob. I'm afraid I've got some bad news.'"

Clearly, this is much gentler than coming straight out with:

"Listen up everyone. Bob's dying."

Make sure you know your limitations. You do not have to have all the answers, nor should you pretend you do. If you don't know something, say so. It is much better than lying or making things up to cover your tracks. Remember, breaking bad news is a very difficult thing to do. Doctors and nurses go on long courses to improve their communication skills and even they don't always get it right. Do not worry if you don't feel adequately prepared. Just do your best.

People don't remember what was said, but they always remember how it was said.

Telling children

Telling children that someone they love is dying can be difficult, and there is no easy way to do it. It is important to remember that a three year old's understanding will differ greatly from a ten year old's. Nevertheless, whatever age they are, children can be very perceptive and will sense that something is wrong. It is often best to be as open and honest with them as you can. If you are not open, children will sense something is wrong and use their imagination – which is always vivid at that young age – to dream up the cause of the distress around them. This can be frightening for them and lead to them not trusting you.

If children are made to feel excluded from what seems to them to be a grown up's problem, they will feel isolated. Sometimes they rationalise things in bizarre ways, perhaps thinking that they are to blame for the person being ill. It is important to reassure them that this is no one's fault and that they have not done anything to cause this. Similarly, now is most definitely not the time to warn them off smoking.

Children often have strange perceptions of what death is and what Heaven is all about. They may ask questions that would be highly inappropriate coming from an adult. They often see things in a more pragmatic way and are less likely to recognise a spiritual dimension to death. Their questions often reflect this.

"When Grandpa is buried, will the wriggly worms eat his body?"

Children often see things in a more pragmatic way and are less likely to recognise a spiritual dimension to death.

Such a question can be highly upsetting for us. It illustrates a distressing dimension to dying that we would try to avoid thinking about. It is vital not to show you are upset and not to get cross with these questions. Children will not understand that they have made a *faux pas* and getting upset will make them feel they cannot ask any more (and there will be many) questions.

Children's minds are constantly developing. Their perception and understanding of illness will change as well. It is inevitable that they will continue to have questions, and it is important that they are given permission to talk to those close to them about a loved one's illness.

It is also useful to warn children about how the illness may affect their loved one. They may need to know that they will be unable to jump on Grandpa's fat belly when they see him next or that Mummy will be too tired to play on the swings with them when she comes home. If these issues are discussed with children, they are more likely to accept them. A sudden refusal to allow them to climb onto Grandpa's lap will cause confusion and feelings of rejection.

"I spent the day dreading picking Lucy up from school, knowing I would have to tell her that her grandmother, my mother, was dying."

"Does that mean I can't go to Brownies tonight?" she asked.

"She was so nonchalant about it, I could have cried."

Although adults respond to devastating news reasonably predictably, children can sometimes surprise us. Having summoned up the courage to tell them the sad news, you may find that children act so matter-of-factly that you question whether they have taken on board anything you have said. This is normal for some children and, given time, they will ask questions as long as they feel they are allowed to.

It is important that any adults that the children may come into contact with are informed of the situation. It is possible that they may choose to open up to someone at school and, if so, they should be given due warning for this. Sadly, schoolchildren can be pretty unpleasant to each other at times. They will focus on a child's perceived weakness, so children may choose to keep family tragedy private from school. Nevertheless, teachers should be made aware of any issues, so that they can offer appropriate support and make allowances for any grieving behaviour.

Children may react in different ways to a loved one's illness. Some behaviour may be difficult to deal with at the best of times, but even more so when you too are going through this difficult time. There are reasons to explain why children react in different ways. It is not just a case of them thinking, *"Now is a good time to get away with being really naughty, 'cos they all feel sorry for me."*

Some children will misbehave atrociously in an attempt to cover up their feelings of insecurity. Others may become withdrawn, spending time away from the rest of the family. This is sometimes out of fear of being hurt or even out of fear that contact with the dying person may rub off on them. Younger children often become very clingy to the ill person or to parents. They may be afraid to leave them in case something happens to them when they are not there.

Dos and don'ts of what to say to children

- Do be as open and honest with them as you can, otherwise they will sense something is wrong and use their imagination to dream up the cause that seems most likely.

- Don't exclude them from what may seem like a grown-up's problem.

- Do reassure them that the illness is not their fault.

- Don't get cross if some of their questions seem tactless. Allow them to keep asking whatever questions they want.

- Do explain how the loved one's illness will affect them.

- Do inform other adults that the children come into contact with.

Telling Teenagers

The first thing to remember about teenagers is this: they are not big children and they are not mini adults either. The best way to view them is as a mixture of both, with different child-like and adult features waxing and waning at unpredictable times.

Being a teenager is awful at the best of times. Your hormones are all over the place, every experience and feeling you have is not only new but it's also unique. Only you understand the problems of the world and it really annoys you that adults, especially your parents, cannot appreciate this.

Mark Twain once wrote *"When I was fourteen I found my father so ignorant, I could hardly bear to have the old man around. Now I am twenty one, I am amazed at how much he has learned in seven years."*

Parents can be so annoying! They don't understand how you feel. They never let you go out when you want to. They don't realise that you are an adult now, and that you will leave home when you are 16. Being a teenager is a really bad time. It is even worse when a loved one is dying. No one tells you anything. As if you aren't mature enough to take the news!

Above all, teenagers need honesty. They need to be treated like adults and given information as you would to an adult. Sometimes, though, they need the support that a child may require. The world that they thought they were at last making sense of suddenly appears to be changing before their very eyes. Teenagers, like children, tend to take their loved ones for granted, especially their parents. If they have been told that they will be losing one of their loved ones, particularly if it is one of their parents, life suddenly feels very unsafe: their rug of security has, in effect, just been pulled from under their feet.

Above all, teenagers need honesty. They need to be treated like adults and given information as you would to an adult.

For that reason, anger is a common response to devastating news and one that is often seen in teenagers. They may be resentful that their loved one will not be around for them anymore. They may feel let down by that person or cross with another member of the family. A mother might take the blame for a grandfather's lung cancer because she should have made him stop smoking. Such reactions are often distressing to cope with.

"When I was 13, my father died. Even though he had been ill for five years, I had no idea how ill he was: when he lost his hair following chemotherapy, I assumed he had gone bald, like all "old men". One morning, I was woken early by my uncle and told that my father had died in the night. As I was closer to my dad than to my mum, I reacted by directing all my anger at my mother, openly wishing she was the one who had died instead. Now I am reconciled with my mother but I am angry instead at my father for denying me the opportunity to round off my relationship with him, and for what he must have put my mother through." **Jessica, 35, recalls her feelings of anger at her father's death.**

Teenagers will often show a level of insight and maturity usually only reserved for the Dalai Lama. Teenagers – and children, it has to be said – have a resilience and a capacity to deal with emotions that should not be underestimated. This is why it is important to explain to them what is going on, so that they can deal with the situation in their own way. Otherwise, they will just sit on their feelings, and it can take years for them to come to terms with that person's death. If the teenagers are losing a parent but are not kept informed or are not able to talk to their loved one, they cannot have any closure, something that can haunt them for many years.

"My mother died when I was 17. Midway through the summer, just weeks before her death, I remember her asking me to buy her some woolly socks, as she would be needing them that winter. I sat there thinking, 'Hang on, I know you're not going to be around, surely you realise you won't be. Why are we going through this charade?' But I still went off and bought the socks. It remains my greatest regret that this gulf of communication remained between us until her death. I did not have the opportunity to say goodbye in any way, to speak to her about my hopes for the future, our lives in the past, and to hug her and feel close to her one final time." **Debbie, 45, wishes she had been able to communicate with her mother.**

Another effect of not giving teenagers clear information about what is happening is that what they are not told, they will fill in. And often, in trying to fill in the blanks in later years, they will assume that things were worse for their loved one than they may well have been because it is their natural instinct to fear what they do not know and to paint a darker picture of what is already a dark area in their lives.

That said, you cannot force a dying person, especially a parent, to talk about their approaching death. You have to respect their wishes and if they do not feel it is right, then nobody should force them to do something that will upset them. They have little enough control over their situation as it is. All you can do is inform them gently about the needs of any children and teenagers but, if they still don't want to talk about it, then that is entirely within their right.

If there are any words of advice for communicating with teenagers they are these: be honest, be available and be supportive. Hope for the best but anticipate the worst. Above all, recognise that all their responses are appropriate responses to a distressing time.

Dos and don'ts of what to say to teenagers

- Do give them clear information about what is going on. What they are not told, they will fill in, often imagining the worst.

- Do continue their routine. Allow them to go out, to have fun, even to have arguments with you!

- Do listen carefully to their emotions, fears, fantasies and questions, however unimportant they may seem.

- Don't protect them from their pain with a conspiracy of silence.

- Do try to get the person who is dying, particularly if it is a parent, to talk to them, and in some ways to round off their relationship.

Different behaviours of the dying person

Just as we have many different emotions when we absorb the news that someone is dying, people who have been told that they are dying may experience some or all of those feelings, as seen in the list below, which mirrors the one on p.54. These emotions will hugely affect how they talk with us and therefore how we will need to communicate with them.

How the person feels will influence how much he or she will want to talk. Some people will not even acknowledge that they are ill or dying. They will show no signs that they want to talk about it. This could be due to many things such as shock or depression. Other people may be keen to talk about things and to acknowledge openly that they know they are dying. Often we find it easier to talk to people who are open about things. It is as if they have given us permission to talk about their illness. When someone does not acknowldge they are dying, it is much harder to know what you can and cannot say.

There is no rule that states that *"Everyone who is dying must open up and talk about how they feel."* Each person will deal with his or her illness in his or her own way.

Each person will deal with his or her illness in his or her own way.

Shock

The shocked person sitting there in stunned silence does not need you to fill the silence with inane banter. Remember how they used to say "*The sign of a true friend is being able to bear the silence*"? Well, this applies in this situation.

"When I was there after being told I was going to die, they said I was silent, that I didn't speak. They may have heard silence but all I could hear was noise. It's just that it was all internal. There was tons going on in my head and when people talked it interrupted me."

This quote captures brilliantly how important it is to listen and not talk too much. Unfortunately we feel that we must say something – after all, we have come all this way. Sometimes people just want someone to sit with them.

Anger

How you talk with someone who is angry with the news may be different from how you talk with someone who is feeling guilty. However, the most important part of communicating with someone in this situation is this: be a good listener.

When your best friend is ranting about how unfair life is and why should it happen to him, he is not expecting you to come up with answers. He is sounding off, trying to make sense of it all and for him, ranting is one way of doing that. Now is not the time to tell him to calm down or pull himself together. He just needs you to be there and to listen. Don't try and come up with the answers – there aren't any. Just listen.

Denial

Sometimes the person may be in denial. Communicating with someone in denial is a difficult thing to do. It is not a straightforward thing where the person says one day, *"I know, I'm going to pretend that I am not dying."* This suggests that it's all a conscious act and that we can get the person to snap out of it or, with gentle persuasion, admit that he or she knew what was going on all along. Denial is actually a very complex coping mechanism whereby the mind convinces itself that everything is OK. In the same way as we immobilise a broken arm in plaster because using it would make things worse, denial is a sort of mechanism to prevent the brain from thinking about awful things too much. True denial is not that common, but it occurs when facing the reality of death is too much to handle. It is important not to aggressively break someone's denial. It is a powerful coping mechanism and interfering with it can cause emotional disarray. It may also be that people who are dying do not want to acknowledge their impending death to those around them because they cannot stand the tone of voice that people adopt around those who are in their situation; they cannot stand the sort of sad, hushed way in which people ask them how they are when they visit. They would prefer people to speak to them in a more normal way. Finally, it may be that, by being in denial about their situation (at least to others), they avoid having to handle other people's fear. They may well feel that it's all they can do to cope with their own, without having to take on that of others.

"Sometimes, in answering well-meant questions, she ends up offering comfort and reassurance to the questioner, which is something that she finds incredibly draining, both physically and mentally." Mandy, whose mother Beryl was dying of cancer.

Sometimes people who are in denial about their death do nonetheless find a subtle way of divulging the fact that they are aware of their situation: they may drop hints about the best place to buy something for a particular relative, where they keep the spare car keys, what their son mentioned he would like for Christmas. This is a way of "handing over", of letting you have information that you may need after their death. It does not mean they want to talk specifically about when they are no longer there, but it does acknowledge that fact, in a way that the dying person can handle emotionally.

"The one time my mother intimated that she knew the end was near, and that she knew that I knew, was when she asked me to change my name when I got a bit older, because she was strangely convinced that my surname might leave me open to anti-semitism from others." Debbie, whose mother died when she was 17.

Fear

We have already explored how we may feel when we hear that a loved one is dying. Some of our own fear is borne from feeling inadequate or unprepared for the problems the future may hold. We fear the unknown because we don't know what to expect. A patient who is dying might be scared for these reasons too. He or she might not know what to expect when he or she dies or might have specific worries. Many people worry that they will experience pain or discomfort at the end. Sometimes people who have breathing difficulties caused, for example, by lung disease or heart failure worry that they will be unable to breathe and will have a feeling of drowning. Fear can be a common emotion for them since breathlessness is a common part of their illness.

For other people, their fear may be due to what we call spiritual distress. Everyone's spirituality is different. The word spirituality is not interchangeable with religion. You can have spiritual needs regardless of whether you believe in a higher being such as God, Allah or Buddha. A person's spirituality is whatever makes them the person that they are and how they interact with the world around them. For a devout Muslim or Christian, for example, it is likely that his or her spirituality is strongly influenced by his or her religion and faith. An atheist or agnostic's spirituality might be influenced by a love of his or her family, a close friend or even a pet. When people are facing death, whether they are religious or not, they are likely to have plenty of time to contemplate their place on this planet and to reflect on their life. They are likely to look back and ask themselves some fairly difficult questions: what have they achieved in their life, how can their life be summed up, what sort of person have they been, and do they have any regrets? They may also worry about the future in terms of "What happens to me now?", "Is there a Heaven and, if so, will I get in?"

Even people who have led their lives with a strong and true faith may fear death. I have witnessed many devout people have crises of faith near the end. Conversely, it is quite common for people who previously had no religious belief, suddenly to discover their faith as their lives draw to a close. In both cases, I do not believe the issue is one of faith; rather, both situations are complex manifestations of fear and anxiety.

Finally, it is also very common for people to fear for the future of those they will leave behind. "Who will care for my children?", "Who will look after my dog?" These are all normal things to worry about and fear. People who are dying may need to talk these things through and explore options with you. Now is the time to be a good listener.

Blame and guilt

When death is imminent, people often experience feelings of "if only". Blame and guilt are complex emotions, which dying people often direct excessively onto themselves and those closest to them. Sometimes these feelings are accompanied by anger. The person may feel angry towards the medical profession:

"Why didn't they pick this up earlier?"

"I knew there was something wrong but no one would listen."

"No one told me what was happening. If I had known I was dying I would have done things sooner."

People are often angry towards those closest to them, not for any particular reason, just because they are nearby – we often hurt the ones we love the most. Sometimes, longstanding problems come to the surface, and grievances are raised at inappropriate moments. Now is not the time to open up old wounds or family feuds. Major grudges that have simmered beneath the surface for years are unlikely to be sorted out by a brief heartfelt speech around the deathbed. It may happen a lot in the movies: feuding families united at the bedside after one beautiful *"Why can't we all get along for the sake of Papa"* speech.

People sometimes feel guilty or blame themselves. They may feel that they should have gone to the doctor earlier, rather than pretend nothing was wrong. They may wish they had given up smoking so they would have more time with their loved ones. When people talk like this they are looking for someone who can listen to them. They are just verbalising their jumble of emotions whilst trying to make sense of them. When talking to someone who is expressing blame or guilt, you will find it is more useful to demonstrate that you are listening and care about what he or she is saying, rather than try to come up with answers that you do not have.

Depression

Depression is very common in people with a terminal illness. At least 60 per cent of people with advanced incurable disease will have some signs of depression. Some people may feel low in mood or tearful but these are just a few ways that depression manifests itself. It can often have physical symptoms (as opposed to psychological ones). People may have poor sleeping patterns and many wake up early and are unable to get back to sleep. Weakness and tiredness, though common in advanced disease, may also be worsened by depression. Depressed people may lose their appetite or desire to do things they previously enjoyed. It is important to understand that depression is not a demonstration of whether or not someone is able to cope. Sadly, because people often think it does betray an inability to cope, they often refuse to acknowledge their low mood.

Depression is partly psychological. It is understandable that a continuous onslaught of bad news and worries will eventually take its toll on the most resilient of us. This is a normal response for our bodies to take when faced with persistent mental trauma. It allows the mind to shut down and recoup. However, there is also a biochemical reason for depression, which helps to explain why it is so common in chronic and terminal diseases. Our body needs certain vitamins and minerals to keep us healthy. Without them we can become unwell. A mineral called *serotonin* is needed to lift and sometimes stabilise our mood. If its levels get low, our mood will drop. Just as a lack of vitamin C can cause skin and gum problems, and a lack of vitamin B12 can cause anaemia, a low level of serotonin can bring on a low mood and depression. The building blocks of serotonin are found in certain food. Chocolate contains lots of these building blocks which probably explains why some women get a chocolate craving when they feel low. A long illness can deplete our body's stores of many important minerals and vitamins, including serotonin. Certain treatments such as an operation or chemotherapy are likely to affect certain mineral levels as well. The bottom line is: people who have been unwell for some time have low levels of serotonin in their blood and for this reason they can get depressed. When someone has a vitamin C deficiency, or has a cold, we give them vitamin C. Anaemic people might be given vitamin B12 or iron. Similarly, there should be no reason not to give someone with a terminal illness a medicine to raise the serotonin level in his or her blood.

Acceptance

Some people accept quite readily that they are dying whilst others refuse to. There is no rule for how one should behave. Sometimes people will only accept what is going on late into their illness. Sometimes this happens after a considerable time talking with close friends and family, and being listened to by them. It may take days or even weeks for people to reconcile themselves to their illness. Some people will never accept what is happening, and that is their prerogative. Some will remain in denial right up until their death. The important thing is that the mental adjustment required to reach the stage of acceptance takes a long time. It does not happen overnight and may only come about after several conversations and opportunities to express how the dying person feels. Do not expect someone's frame of mind to shift after one chat with you or one session with professional help.

Relief

Not everyone will experience all the feelings mentioned in this list. The aim was not to be a "tick box exercise", nor to identify which emotion your loved one had yet to go through. It doesn't work like that. The purpose of the list of emotions is to help you to understand that the responses your loved one may demonstrate are entirely normal.

Some people experience relief when they near the end of their life. They may feel that everything has been taken care of, that all their affairs are in order, and that they can rest in peace now. Some may have had such bad experiences with their illness that they view death as a welcome relief from their suffering. Whatever the reason for the feeling of relief experienced by dying people, it usually brings with it an accompanying sense of reassurance and relief in those closest to them.

Visiting someone who is dying

If you are going to visit someone who is dying, the chances are he or she will be in one of the following places –

- hospital
- hospice
- nursing home
- their own home (or family member's home).

The pros and cons of being cared for in hospital or in a hospice are covered in detail in Chapter 3. However, people might be looked after in a different place from where they eventually die. A hundred years ago, most people died at home, whilst now the majority of deaths take place in hospital. Hospitals, hospices and nursing homes may run and function slightly differently from each other. It is worth being aware of a few things when you visit each of these places.

It may feel abnormal

Unless you are a healthcare professional, going to a hospital – and even more so to a hospice – is not a normal experience. For some people, it can be positively daunting. The visit may bring back difficult memories or feelings.

The person you are visiting may not look as they normally do. You may never have seen your loved one with teeth out, or make-up not done. The person may have lost weight or seem more tired than usual. He or she may be in bed rather than up and about as you remember him or her. It is inevitable that things will appear "not normal".

If you are visiting someone at his or her home, things may also feel strange. Often when people come home from hospital, they are not strong enough to care for themselves. They may not be able to get up the stairs. Sometimes people have their bed moved downstairs so they don't need to go up and down the stairs all day. Often, they are sent home on different medicines. These might be in tablet or syrup form and you might see them around the house. On occasions, people have medicines given as a continuous slow injection under the skin. This is given via a small medicine pump called a syringe driver – a very small medicine pump, no bigger than a personal stereo.

Visiting regulations

Most hospitals and hospices have visiting hours, and it is important to know when these are to avoid going to all the effort of calling in on someone, only to discover that visiting is not for another two hours. There are reasons for visiting times, and these are primarily for the patients' benefit. When people are ill, they often need more rest and sleep and a constant succession of callers will prevent patients from resting. Visits can often tire patients out because they make an effort to "appear well" for those who have made such an effort to come and see them.

This does not mean that a dying person cannot have someone with him or her outside visiting hours. Far from it. Nursing staff will do everything they can to allow close families to stay with their loved one once they become really unwell. Indeed, some wards, and especially those in hospices, may not have visiting times at all.

Considering other patients

Unless you are visiting your loved one at his or her home, there will almost certainly be other patients around when you visit. Some of them may be as unwell as the person you are visiting, perhaps even more so. Some patients are looked after in a ward, usually with four to six beds in a room. Sometimes people are looked after in a side room. Often, when someone is dying, the family and patient will be offered a side room for privacy. There is nothing worse than feeling everyone else on the ward is watching you at this sad time. However, this does not mean that if a loved one is moved into a side room that they are dying! There are many clinical reasons why people in hospitals are given side rooms. Sometimes it is because of infections or because the patient's immune system is not good. A side room is not synonymous with dying.

People who are together on a ward often become friendly and have a chat across the room. They may get to know each other's families when they visit. It helps to be mindful that other people on the ward will be affected by the news that someone is dying, not just because it is sad, but also because it reminds them of their illness and fears for the future.

Also these people have needs as well. They may need to rest and be in a quiet environment. Be careful not to disturb other people. Bringing young children to see Grandpa is lovely but children get bored quickly. It is unfair on other patients if children are left to run up and down the ward whilst you get down to a heart to heart with your dad.

Other visitors

When someone is ill, true friends show themselves. People are often surprised by how kind and considerate others can be. There are often many thoughtful people who send their best wishes or who come and pay a visit. When visiting, the patient is the number one priority. We are fulfilling their needs not our own. Therefore, do not resent other people from popping in. Try not to hog all the visiting time, since that will prevent others from visiting. There is usually a maximum number of people allowed to visit at any one time and it is often better if people take turns. This is especially the case when the person has entered the terminal phase, when they are rarely awake. It is important at that stage that people take it in turns to be at the bedside, because a side room full of people will quickly get very warm and stuffy. This will then make things uncomfortable for the ill person, and can make them appear unsettled and possibly even agitated.

Practicalities of visiting a dying person

The aim of this section is to give some practical advice for someone who is planning on visiting a dying person. Some of the information may seem obvious, but when we are already worried about visiting someone, we sometimes forget simple things that we would normally have thought of, so what follows is meant as a reminder, should your mind already be occupied by other things.

Timing

Correctly planning the timing of visiting a dying person is essential. The questions you need to consider are as follows:

Do I need to see him or her immediately? I know many people who continue to feel incredibly guilty because they didn't get to see their loved one before he or she died.

"No one told me Dad was going to die that quickly. I had planned to come down that weekend with the children but he died before we got down. If I had known that he only had a few days to live I would have dropped everything and been there straight away."

Unfortunately it is difficult be specific about how long someone has to live. Even the most experienced doctors and nurses will be unable to give you an accurate prediction. The best they can do is give you a ball park figure based on their best guess. It is reasonable to ask them whether you are looking at hours, days or weeks, so that you can make plans to have time off work and to alert loved ones. Even so, a terminal illness can often follow an unpredictable course and it sometimes catches people out. However, unless the professionals involved in the dying person's care have indicated that you need to come down straight away, you usually have time to visit. It is important to know, though, that the professionals will only advise you to come in immediately if you have expressed a wish to be informed if things take a turn for the worse.

What time of the day should I go and see them? Assuming that your visit is not an urgent one as described above, it is hoped that you are able to plan your visit so that it is as convenient as possible and as nice as possible for the loved one. Many wards will limit visiting hours for reasons already explained, but when a patient is dying, they tend to relax the rules so that loved ones can be present all the time if need be.

If someone has already visited, it's a good idea to ask their advice when to visit. Otherwise, find out directly from the loved one: when would he or she like you to visit? Some people are at their best in the mornings after a good rest, but get progressively tired as the day goes on. Other people feel groggy in the mornings but pick up for a few hours in the evening. Some people may feel slightly nauseated as the day progresses but are on great form at midday.

How long should I stay? It doesn't matter if you have spent six hours in a car to come and visit someone, only for them to say, after ten minutes, that they need a sleep. It doesn't matter how much effort you have gone to to visit the dying person. Remember, this is not about you, it's about them. It is often better to do a few short visits. Some families spend time with their loved one, go off for a cup of tea somewhere, then return a few hours later. That way the loved one will be able to rest but still enjoy visitors.

Remember, this is not about you, it's about them.

How often should I visit? There are two things to consider here: your own needs and the loved one's. Knowing someone you care for is dying is devastating. You may need to spend as much time as possible with that person, knowing that every moment is precious and about to be taken from you. But the needs of dying people are also important. They may have their own views on how often they want visitors. Don't forget that other people will want to visit as well. Try to coordinate visits so that you do not have hoards of people descending on your loved one at the same time.

Where to sit

There are usually visitors' chairs in hospitals and hospices. Make sure they are placed in a position where you can be seen and heard without the dying person having to make an effort or get uncomfortable as the visit progresses. If the person you are visiting has poor hearing in one ear, sit on the good side. Sometimes people like to sit on the bed. This is nice: it's intimate and close. But always check that this is OK with the person being visited. Sometimes people may appear comfortable in bed but a slight movement can cause them considerable pain. Also, look around you to make sure you are not disturbing any medicines or equipment. People may have medicines on their table or drinks close by. They may be hooked up to a drip or syringe driver, which you must be careful not to disturb.

Gifts

Clichéd though it sounds, the best gift you can give someone who is dying is your time, empathy and availability. However, we often like to bring something as a token of affection. The old favourites such as chocolates, grapes and flowers may not be appropriate in this situation. Dying people sometimes suffer from nausea and arriving with a bowl of fruit and some chocolates may worsen that feeling. Some wards are unkeen to have flowers on the ward for various reasons, so it is best to check first. A card and best wishes are often enough. Remember, when you see the loved one, you can ask if they would like you to bring anything. It is much better to get or do something that the person really needs.

… the best gift you can give someone who is dying is your time …

What to say

As explained at the start of the chapter, it is not possible to give a set script that can be used when talking to someone who is dying. Neither is it possible to give insightful words of wisdom, which can be reeled off to make someone happy with their condition. If anything, the most helpful thing to guide you when talking to someone who is dying is a list of general dos and don'ts. Most importantly, so long as you avoid the don'ts you should be fine!

Dos and don'ts of communication

- Do be yourself
- Do be honest
- Do be comfortable with silence
- Do accept that different people are good at different things
- Do recognise your strengths
- Don't avoid the person
- Don't make promises that you can't keep
- Don't make crass comments
- Don't overstay your welcome

Be yourself

This refers to one of the "touchstones of normality" that the dying need from others. This friend or loved one just wants you to be you. He or she is not expecting you to come charging in on a white horse to make it all better. He or she just wants you as you are. If you are visiting an old fishing pal, be prepared to talk a bit about fishing trips you have been on recently. If you went to watch the football together, have a chat about the match. Even better, go round and watch the football together. Often, when people are unwell, they miss doing normal things. You can be a conduit to that normality. If you try to be something that you are not and start behaving differently from how you normally behave, they will really be thrown by you. Naturally, a degree of sensitivity is required. If your relationship has been built on mock banter of jokey insults and abuse, it is probably not appropriate to continue this line when you visit.

"Please, all of you out there, let me do it this way. Don't ask "How are you feeling today?", because it's, as always, pretty rough. It's scary and not something I want to dwell on, be reminded of or talk about. I'm still the same Beryl that I was two weeks ago, two months ago, and two years ago. Treat me as you always have, please. As a friend who wants to know all the gossip and wants to have a laugh. And as a friend who will listen to your problems and aches and pains, as I always have. In this way, I promise, you will help me in the best way that you can."

Beryl, who was dying of cancer, wrote the above letter to all her friends, telling them how they could best help her.

Be honest

"One of the girls from work came to see me. She said to me, 'I really don't know what to say, but I just wanted you to know I'm really sorry you're ill.' That's all I needed to hear. We then had a lovely chat."

Being honest is all about being you again. Patients often feel that no one gives them a straight answer anymore. Don't be one of those people. A degree of honesty gives the person more control of their surroundings again. If he or she feels that you are not giving straight answers or are putting up barriers, he or she won't feel able to talk to you about other matters. No one is expecting you to be a hero. They are expecting you to be you.

No one is expecting you to be a hero. They are expecting you to be you.

Be comfortable with silence

"What I like about Joe is he doesn't say much when he visits. He just listens. When I'm feeling tired, it takes a bit longer for me to get my thoughts together and say things. With Joe I don't feel rushed and I can say what I want at my pace."

We all hate uncomfortable silences. We have this uncontrollable urge to say something rather than sit quietly. Often that's when we say crass or silly things because we feel we should be saying something.

Silence is not a bad thing. For one, it shows the loved one that you are listening. He or she is more likely to talk about how he or she feels if given the chance. It shows him or her that what he or she has to say is important. Often, when people are talking about a problem, they are not looking for answers, they just want to verbalise how they feel. Sometimes just getting something out in the open is therapy enough. Don't feel under pressure to come up with answers or solutions you don't have.

Accept other people's strengths

"When Mum was ill, I know it sounds terrible but I really resented my brother for being so good at communicating. I think I was jealous that she talked more openly to him than to me. Looking back now, I'm just glad she had someone she could talk to."

It is a human trait to want to be needed. Part of us likes to be the one people turn to in a crisis, and it is good that you make yourself available. Remember, though, this is not a competition. Your loved one will turn to different people for different things. He or she may confide in one friend about money worries and another about being scared of dying. Remember, it is your loved one's illness, his or her death. He or she can talk to whoever he or she wants to about it. It's not a popularity contest. If you feel your loved one is not opening up to you, don't make a fuss. He or she has enough worries without needing to sort out your bruised pride. Just be glad he or she is talking to someone.

Recognise your strengths

You wouldn't try to build a house if you had no experience at it. Similarly, you wouldn't try to fix the brakes on your car. We tend to know our limitations when it comes to practical things, but often when it comes to a loved one who is ill, we all become experts. We all have opinions on which medicines will work. We act as if we have a PhD in psychology and human behaviour and will readily give advice to that effect.

Why do we do this? Well, part of it is that we feel helpless and want to do something. We hate sitting around doing nothing. We can't bear the idea that we have no control over the situation, that we can't just make things better by taking a different medicine, or seeing another doctor. The fact is that, however hard we try, this time it won't make any difference to the eventual outcome, and that is a very hard thing to accept, particularly when it comes to the life of our nearest and dearest. The other thing is that, by being human, we all understand a little about psychology and human behaviour. We all know people who have been ill and have taken such and such a medicine. Sometimes, however, we get it very wrong. We often give opinions based on our experience of other people with an illness but forget that each person's case is unique.

"Mrs Jenkins down the road had heart failure last year but she's fine now. These doctors can't know what they're doing."

"I see they've got you on that strong pain killer. I wouldn't take it. My aunt took that and it made her really ill."

There will be things you are good at and things you are not so good at. Play to your strengths. Are you the sort who can make sure the cat is OK or take the children to school? Can you do some washing or give lifts to people who can't drive? It is often people who offer the simple bits of support that have the greatest impact on our lives.

"If you could do something that would really help, please offer to help her with everyday jobs that she just can't manage: putting the laundry on, ironing, putting the rubbish out, doing a bit of shopping, even changing a light bulb could be exactly what she needs."

Mandy, Beryl's daughter, wrote a letter to her mother's friends, letting them know how they could best help her mother during her final months.

Don't avoid the person

"You know what? The thing that strikes me the most is not the friends who have been there for me, it's the friends who haven't. People I have known for years have avoided me in the street. It's as if I'm some leper or something."

You would not believe how many people say something like this. People who are dying are not expecting you to offer groundbreaking words of wisdom, just acknowledge they are ill and that you are sorry. Sending a card and offering availability is all you need to do. You may not get another chance and will not be able to put it right when they are gone.

Don't make promises you can't keep

Time can go pretty slowly when people are unwell. Often they are not up to watching TV and don't feel well enough to read. They look forward to people popping in, and if they know someone is coming round, they will get up specially, maybe put on some make-up or get their hair done. They might even get some extra rest in for a few days so they can be on good form the day that someone visits. That day you promised to visit and didn't? Well, they got up especially to see you and felt let down that you didn't show. Someone who is dying may be swimming in a lake of disappointment and regret. Do not add to it.

Sometimes we offer to do things that we cannot deliver on because we are snowed under with other commitments. You meant to visit but you had to get the kids to school and then the car needed taking to the garage and you had promised to take your mother out shopping. Sometimes we take on more than we can handle and something has to give. No matter how small a commitment seems to us, it is better not to make that promise if we have too much on already. Other people will be available to help out if asked. You cannot be all things to all people.

Don't make crass comments

The reason most of us feel uncomfortable talking to people who are dying is because it is a sad situation and we feel helpless that we are unable to do anything about it. We wish we could say something to make it better. The fact is we can't. Unless you know that the dying person is in denial about their illness, in which case they do not want you to be honest about the situation, the next time you feel like saying one of the following, think about why you feel the need to say it.

"I'm sure you'll be fine."

In reality, you know the person won't be fine. *You* know you're talking nonsense. He or she knows you're talking nonsense. What you have effectively done is put up a barrier to any further meaningful conversation. This may be out of fear and denial on your part, and/or an unwillingness to be honest about the situation. But the fact is, you have probably not helped the dying person.

"You're a fighter. You'll be OK."

This may sound nice and in some ways it is meant as a compliment. There is also a commonly held view that, if a patient fights hard enough, he or she can "win the battle" against the illness. But this sort of comment is often unhelpful because it can also put a lot of pressure on people to get better. If they die now does that mean they didn't fight hard enough? They have enough on their hands without feeling guilty and a failure for not having "fought hard enough" in the eyes of those around them.

"You're looking much better. You'll be up and around in no time. Mark my words."

Once again, you don't really believe this. You are just trying to say something hopeful because you feel uncomfortable. There is an argument that we should remain optimistic because the power of positive thinking is important. That is true and should not be underestimated. However, we should also recognise that sometimes these words can act as barriers to important conversations.

"I mentioned to my husband that I felt less well today. 'Nonsense,' he replied. 'You're going to be fine. You're a fighter.' Every time I try to open up, he tells me not to be silly. There are things we need to discuss, but each time he says something like that I don't feel I can."

Don't overstay your welcome

If you are one of those people who feels comfortable visiting and talking to someone who is ill, you will recognise the benefit people can get from a visit and a chat. However, it's a bit like rich fruitcake: a little bit is really nice but too much is unbearable.

Patients will do their utmost to be on their best form for visitors. However, this can be tiring. That's why nurses in hospitals often limit the number of visitors. It is much better to visit frequently for short periods of time than spend ages there. The best thing to do is to say that you don't want to tire the person out and would he or she like you to stay for a bit longer or go? Do try, though, to gauge if, when the person urges you to stay, he or she is simply being too polite to tell you to go!

Don't suffer just to show you care

"I don't care how much it costs. I am prepared to sell the house to get this cured."

When a loved one is ill we will do anything to help. We would gladly swap places with that person, to avoid his or her suffering. The other reason we would want to swap is so that we no longer feel terrible and helpless at being unable to help.

Many of us deal with problems in a very practical way. When Humpty Dumpty fell off the wall, the King didn't recognise that Humpty was likely to die from his injuries. He got all his horses and all his men to try to fix him. This turned out to be futile, although the King probably felt a bit better because he felt he had done *something*. What Humpty really needed was someone to make him feel comfortable, check he wasn't distressed and maintain his dignity.

This analogy may sound flippant. It is not meant to be. It is meant to illustrate that sometimes, despite all our efforts and best intentions, people die. We need to recognise this, otherwise we will concentrate all our energy on trying to find practical solutions to futile situations. Remortgaging the house to fund a trip to America for a new drug that has a five per cent chance of working may seem the right thing to do. But ask yourself this: do you really believe that this new drug is going to work? Could the time spent raising the money and flying to America be better spent in other ways? Sometimes these ventures are right. They are inspiring. They give us hope. But sometimes they shield us from accepting that there is really nothing else that can be done and we should focus on quality time with our loved one.

Sometimes we almost feel we need to put ourselves out for someone so much that we in turn suffer in some way. By doing this we feel we are showing this loved one how much we care. Just remember that when your loved one is gone, you will still be here picking up the pieces. It is important to have emotional, physical and financial reserves to get you through the sad times that come later.

Visiting with children and teenagers

This can often be a source of much worry for us. We may worry that it is inappropriate to have our children visit a dying person for fear that it will disturb or upset the children. Likewise, we may worry that a visiting child or teenager may be upsetting or disturbing for the person being visited. The truth is that everyone will react differently and you may not be able to predict how these visits will go. The most important person in this is the dying person, so his or her views need to be taken into account first. Would he or she like his or her nephew to come and visit? If the dying person would like visits from children or young adults, the next consideration is for those visiting.

As we have mentioned before, one of the most upsetting things for children and teenagers in this situation is feeling excluded from what is going on. They are unlikely to understand that, if you choose to "protect" them from the sadness around them, you are doing it because you feel it is for the best. From their point of view, they feel in a position to decide what they are able to cope with, and not involving them may precipitate resentment and a complex ongoing bereavement. It is much better to be open with them from the start and allow them to decide if they want to come along.

The first visit with a child or teenager should be viewed specifically as a visit for that younger person. Now is not the time to have a long and meaningful chat with your loved one, whilst trying to keep your eye on an escaping toddler. Be prepared to cut the visit short if the children get restless or are disturbing other patients. Children have less concept of time (other than it seems longer) and are likely to get bored after a few minutes. They are unlikely to understand that this may be the last time they see their loved one. It is often useful to forewarn the children what to expect when they visit. Let them know what the ward looks like, if there are any strange machines on the ward. Contrary to belief, young children tend to be more fascinated than scared by such things. Warn children that their loved one may not look how they usually do because they feel unwell. Sometimes it is useful relating back to times when they themselves felt ill and looked poorly. It is also advisable, if visiting a hospital or hospice, to tell them that there may be other unwell people around and that they will need to be good and not disturb them. In practice, a child on a ward brightens up visiting time for most people there.

Teenagers may wish to have time on their own with the dying person. They should be given the opportunity to have some privacy if they need it.

Saying goodbye

Once again, films have a lot to answer for. So many movie deaths are beautifully choreographed. You know how it goes: the person holds on just long enough to speak to his or her loved one. The loved one looks into the dying person's eyes as he or she mutters some deeply moving and profound words that cross boundaries, heal wounds and build emotional bridges with which to face the future. The dying person then stares ahead for a few brief seconds before turning his or her head away, maintaining open eyes. If he or she is holding a trinket or paperweight in his or her hand, he or she will release it to fall gently to the ground. A favourite pet such as the dog, who has remained silent throughout this farewell will gently scratch at the bed, whimpering. Although the Hollywood death is in some ways comforting and beautiful, it creates a myth of the way we die and also that we should somehow say all the things we need to say at the deathbed.

The truth of the matter is that near the end, people do not always know that they are dying. Yes, they know that they are going to die soon, but not that they are going to die within the next 24 hours. It is very hard to say all those fond farewells and final words unless both parties are aware that these words are final. So what should we say? When should we say it?

… why wait until that loved one is on his or her deathbed before we say all those things we have wanted to say?

Life is precious and none of us knows when we or someone we care about will die. Some loved ones are taken from us suddenly without warning: by a massive heart attack or a horrible accident. Some loved ones die after a period of serious illness. Death does not discriminate and we all know of young healthy people cut down in their prime. We sometimes grieve more for young people who die, in the belief that it is more acceptable for old people to go, since they have had a long life. The bottom line is, death is rubbish, no matter what age you are, and none of us can accurately predict when the person we love the most will be taken from us. Therefore, why wait until that loved one is on his or her deathbed before we say all those things we have wanted to say? Say them now while you are both well. There is no need to make a major speech, going through your list of things you want to cover; just let people you care about know, before it's too late. When you are sitting by your mother's bedside having been called by the hospital, you do not want to be filled with regrets.

Do those things now, while your loved ones are alive and well. Hopefully, then, when you are with them at the end, you won't be filled with "what ifs" and "if onlys". You will feel sad but reconciled that there is nothing you need to say at this time because it has all been said already. At a tragic time such as this, it can be a comforting thought.

One final thing. When someone hears devastating news such as being told they are going to die, they will be upset by it. BAD NEWS IS BAD NEWS. It is normal to respond to devastating news with tears and crying. One of the major obstacles to talking openly with a dying person is a fear we will upset him or her. We will go to great lengths to avoid saying anything that might make that person cry. We pick our words carefully. We talk about positive things. We try to take the loved one's mind off things and if he or she starts to cry, it's "OH MY GOD WHAT HAVE I DONE!" But all you have done is allow a distressed person to express an appropriate emotional response to a horrible situation.

Remember when you heard bad news that turned you cold? Remember that feeling of restraint? "*I must not cry. Hold it together. Don't let them see me cry.*" We almost see crying as a weakness and, if someone cries in front of us, we think we must have been really insensitive to make them tearful. Let me suggest another thing. Crying is normal. If you are with someone who starts crying, take it as a high compliment, that they feel comfortable enough in your company to let you see them at their most open and emotionally exposed. Resist the temptation to panic. Resist the urge to say something crass like "*Don't worry, I'm sure you'll be fine,*" because this invalidates the person's distress. It sends a message to them that their distress is uncalled for and that they should not be reacting like this. Avoid empty reassurances that you cannot really deliver. Just remember this:

BAD NEWS IS BAD NEWS. WE CANNOT MAKE IT GOOD NEWS.

What the dying person needs now is for you to be comfortable with his or her sadness; to acknowledge that the news is upsetting and that you are there for him or her whatever happens, and you will do whatever is in your power to do.

Chapter 3 **Caring for someone who is dying**

We experience all sorts of emotions when we learn of the pending death of a loved one. It is difficult not to go into complete psychological meltdown and not to want to hide from the world outside. Yet, now is the time we need to be as strong as possible. There are practicalities that may need addressing, in particular where the loved one wishes to die, and how best they can be cared for in the intervening time. It is possible that the loved one will turn to you for help in these matters. There are various care options that are available, depending on whether the dying person is in a hospital, hospice or in their own home. There are also some new initiatives in the NHS that have been developed to try to ensure that all people receive the same standard of care at the end of life. Finally, it must be acknowledged that when faced with a terminal diagnosis, some people think about, and even request, euthanasia.

Options for care

When the doctors inform someone that their illness is incurable, they have come to that assessment after considerable deliberation and thought. They do their best to consider reversible causes of the patient's deterioration and to treat them accordingly. They only come to the conclusion that someone is dying once other options have been ruled out. Hopefully, this will reassure you that your loved one has not been put on the scrap heap, that the hospital hasn't just given up on them. If anything, in reality, the reverse is probably true: medical teams sometimes decide the patient is dying later than they should. Families are then relieved to be given the news because it confirms what they thought had been happening for days.

When doctors acknowledge that someone is dying, the prime consideration is to make sure they are symptom-free and to maintain their dignity. Teams do their best to avoid putting a patient through tests or treatments that will not alter the outcome; rather, they will focus their care on comfort measures. To put the problem another way, ask yourself the following question: if you were given a week to live before you died with cancer, would you –

a   want to spend quality time with your loved ones?

b   opt for chemotherapy, which might make you sick and may not help you live longer?

When looked at this way, most of us would take option "a". We would take the option that would give us the best quality of life. However, when facing death, having been told that there are no further treatments available, many of us say, in fact, that we are prepared to try anything, no matter how bad the odds are.

Getting a second opinion

It is tempting to ask for a second opinion. That is entirely your right. But before you do, consider this: do you want a second opinion because you think your current doctor doesn't know his stuff, or is it because you are desperate to show your loved one that you care so much that you will leave no stone unturned to find a cure? There have been times, it is true, when, through the sheer determination of loved ones, other treatment options have been found for terminally ill patients and they have responded to the 1000 to 1 shot. However, for every story such as this, there are a thousand that have not turned out that way. Even sadder is the fact that the time spent by the family in a futile search for a cure was time they could have spent with their loved one facing the future together, reconciling the end of life and demonstrating their love in a wordless act of just being there. Another thing to consider is that most decisions these days are made by a team of health professionals and not by one mightier-than-thou consultant. Cases are discussed in multidisciplinary team meetings (MDTs) and treatment options are reached by consensus, according to established guidelines. There are clear rules that govern the delivery of health care, and ensure it is standardised across the United Kingdom, so you should get the same treatment for a condition in Cardiff as you would in Coventry. This is not to say that the National Health Service is wonderful, perfect and flawless, but you should be reassured that any concerns you might have about a loved one's care, and especially about the decision-making process, are usually unfounded.

In summary, it is not the case that a second opinion should not be sought if you feel that one is warranted; just be careful not to go chasing futile goals when time is precious and would be better spent in the "now".

How to assess care options

When considering options of care, once the chance of recovery has been ruled out, there are a few things you need to think about, especially if you are planning to take someone home.

The patient is unlikely to improve much from now If someone was walking about two weeks ago, for example, but has now become so unwell that he or she is unable to get out of bed, that person is unlikely to be well enough to get on his or her feet again. This is an important consideration when planning future care because returning to an environment that was manageable when the person was well, may not be manageable now. Things like getting up the stairs or having a bath unaided will be difficult.

The patient is likely to deteriorate progressively If someone is just about able to get out of bed and get to the toilet today, he or she may not be able to do it tomorrow. When people are dying, they become weaker and weaker. In planning someone's care, you must plan for how they will be at their least well. In practical terms, this means planning for someone who will be bed bound at the end.

Being the main carer for someone isn't easy This is not said to try to put you off from doing it. Looking after someone for 24 hours a day is hard work. Nurses do an excellent job, but at least they have been formally trained to be nurses. What's more they can go home after a shift, and leave work behind. As a carer you don't have that luxury. The other thing that should be recognised is that not all of us are able to care for our loved ones in a way we would wish. This does not mean we should be viewed in a poor light. Saying you are unable to provide the hands-on care that a dying patient might require is in some ways a very brave and caring thing to do. It recognises your own limitations and that you want care to be delivered by those who are better qualified.

The other thing that can happen is that during the final stages of the dying person's life, relatives want to concentrate on being a loved one – a wife, a daughter, a son, a husband – and not a physical hands-on carer. This is an important distinction. The reverse can also be true, of course: other families have felt it is their right and their privilege to look after the dying person.

Getting the best from the professionals

At a time when you have been told that time is limited and that every day is precious, it is unbelievable how long it can take sometimes to get things done in hospital. Waiting for a bed in a hospice or getting everything in place so that a loved one can safely be discharged home all takes time. Unfortunately, time is something we do not have much of, and we can become very frustrated when things do not seem to be going to plan. What is the best way to get the best out of health professionals? How do you get things moving along smoothly?

Whatever you do, avoid losing your temper with the staff looking after your loved one. You may feel better for a few minutes but it will not help your loved one and, if anything, it may even be very unhelpful. The chances are you are getting angry with someone who is in no way connected to your loved one's case, and your rant will do no more than upset a complete stranger. Sadly, NHS staff are exposed to more aggression and violence in the workplace than ever before, and Trusts operate a zero tolerance policy with respect to such behaviour. Healthcare professionals recognise that when a loved one is ill, people become upset, but this in no way excuses aggressive behaviour.

To get the best out of the people looking after your loved one, there are a few things to consider that might be of help.

Identify the key worker A key worker is the person who will take responsibility for the coordination of your loved one's care. It may be one of the doctors, such as the Senior House Officer (SHO), or perhaps a particular nurse who is coordinating the next aspect of care. With respect to choosing a place of care for a patient, people such as the hospital social worker, Specialist Palliative Care Nurse or discharge coordinator will be involved. Other members of a multidisciplinary team such as physiotherapists and occupational therapists will also have input as appropriate. The nursing documentation should identify who the key worker is. This is the person with whom you should most keep in contact.

Nominate a main spokesperson for the family It is very helpful when discussing options of care to have one nominated family member through which all communication is handled. Imagine for one moment that a ward has 24 patients and each family has one relative. If each relative needs to have a discussion with the doctor that lasts at least five minutes (in reality this can take much longer), then two hours of the doctor's working day will be taken up talking to relatives. In an average working day of eight hours, this will leave six hours to look after patients (assuming the doctor has no lunch or tea break). Imagine now that each patient has four children who all visit at different times and all want to talk to the doctor. Now the doctor will spend eight hours talking to relatives. When will the doctor look after the patients? Rather than take up a professional's time to repeat the same information, it is better for all involved to have a key spokesperson and point of contact for the family.

Arrange specific times to discuss issues It is much better to arrange a specific time to discuss things. For your part, it means you do not have to hang around, hoping the person will come on the ward by chance. From the professional's point of view, they are not caught "on the hop" and can check your loved one's case prior to the meeting in case there is any new information.

Think about what information you need Some people forget what questions they were going to ask when they meet the healthcare worker. It is well worth writing down a list of things you want to ask. If you don't, the chances are you will remember the question the minute the person has left.

Ask what you can do to help Sometimes there are things that you can do to help with the care planning for a dying person. Ask if there is anything you can do as a family to help things move along more quickly. Offer to make yourself available to meet with social workers, occupational therapists and other such people. If your loved one has chosen to be looked after in a care home, why not go and visit some to see which are most suitable?

Liaise with community services Keep in contact with your loved one's GP. If the practice is aware that a patient is due to come home soon, they will start putting things in place to make this happen. The district nurse will be alerted that she will need to be involved. Specialist equipment such as hospital beds can be booked. This should all happen anyway, but it is amazing how useful it can be to liaise with the relevant people yourself.

If all else fails, request an appointment with the consultant Ninety nine times out of a hundred, the NHS gets it right and the planning of care for a patient runs smoothly. Sometimes things do not go to plan, however, and this can be for several reasons. Sometimes it is due to a failure of the system within the NHS, sometimes it is due to a simple oversight (so-called human error) and sometimes (thankfully rarely) it is because the team have not got themselves organised quickly enough. In this situation, it is worth requesting an appointment to speak with the consultant in charge. Do this calmly and politely. At the appointment, state clearly what has been going on and enquire what options are available to resolve the current difficulties. The consultant will be keen to see the problem resolved.

NHS versus private care

When a loved one is ill, we do all we can to show that we care. We do anything to help, even if it makes us suffer in some way. Families often ask if it would be possible to move a loved one to a private hospital. This is always possible but there are three main things that need to be considered first:

What will a private hospital offer that an NHS will not? Private hospitals vary across the country, but by and large they have a huge expertise in managing common medical and surgical conditions that are non life-threatening. Private hospitals are very experienced at looking after "well" people. They have less experience at looking after dying patients, especially complex cases. Few private hospitals have resident MacMillan Nurses, for example; few have Palliative Care Consultants either. Although the environment is nice, the expertise is not as developed. If you are not convinced, do this simple test: get on the internet and look up your local private hospital. There will be a list of consultants and their specialties. Look up orthopaedic surgeons. There will be hundreds of them. Now look up Palliative Medicine Consultant ...

Financial considerations If you have a health care plan for private treatment, check whether it provides palliative care, and what that care entails. Some plans offer stays in palliative care beds in private care homes. However, if your health plan does not cover this, a bed in a private hospital is likely to be very expensive if the loved one has more than a few days to live.

Expertise If you want to move your loved one to a private hospital, he or she will be under a named consultant. As previously mentioned, not that many Palliative Medicine Consultants have private practices, so your loved one is unlikely to be under the care of someone whose day-to-day work involves care of the dying. This doesn't mean that other doctors cannot offer effective terminal care to patients, it just means that if you pay to go private, you pay to get treated by the specialist. To put it another way, if you paid for a cardiology opinion and you were seen by a Palliative Medicine Physician, you wouldn't be too happy. The same applies for end-of-life care.

Liverpool Care of the Dying Pathway (LCP)

In almost every area of clinical care, health care professionals will encounter death or its aftermath. Nurses report that a "bad" death can have a lasting impact and leave staff feeling powerless to cope with future death-related issues. A "good" death can transform practice, improve morale and impact on future ability to care. It can shape a nurse's career. In hospitals it can be particularly difficult to recognise when a patient has entered the dying phase. The shift of focus from that of cure to that of symptom control and ongoing care in the last weeks and days of life can be the most challenging time for a ward team, and educational support in this area of care is generally poor.

It is important to realise that most nursing and medical staff are motivated to provide quality care to patients in the last days or hours of life and that there are often specific factors beyond their control that cause the care of dying patients to be less than adequate. These include lack of appropriate education, "busyness", lack of resources and an inappropriate ward environment.

The aim of the Liverpool Care of the Dying Pathway (LCP) is to empower doctors and nurses to deliver high quality care to dying patients and their relatives. It facilitates multiprofessional communication and documentation and integrates national guidelines. It provides demonstrable outcomes for care of the dying, and should reduce and inform complaints commonly associated with this area of care.

What is an Integrated Care Pathway?

Integrated Care Pathways are used widely throughout the health care system. A pathway determines locally agreed, multidisciplinary practice based on guidelines and evidence, where available, for a specific patient/user group. It forms all or part of the clinical record, it documents the care given and facilitates the evaluation of outcomes for continuous improvement.

There are key elements that constitute a care pathway –

- it organises the process
- there is a timeline element
- there is supportive evidence of practice
- there is an element of multidisciplinary collaboration
- there are elements of care identified, usually within an agreed timeframe
- there is a continuous review of practice
- there is an assessment of variance
- it is focused on outcome
- it constitutes all or part of the clinical record
- the pathway should inform risk and benefit.

What is the LCP?

The Liverpool Care of the Dying Pathway is an Integrated Care Pathway designed to guide the delivery of care in the last hours/days of life. It was developed through the expertise of health care professionals with knowledge and expertise of caring for patients within the hospice setting. It transfers the key aspects of this care into the LCP to enable education and empowerment of hospital staff who can then deliver high quality care for dying patients. Key areas that were identified for inclusion in the document were:

Identifying patients who are to be included in the pathway The diagnosis of dying is made by the multiprofessional team caring for the patient and is dependent on the exclusion of reversible or treatable causes of the patient's condition. It is often associated with the patient being bedridden, semi-comatose, only able to take sips of fluid and unable to swallow tablets. It is important to recognise that a diagnosis of dying is not absolute and, at times, the patient's condition can improve and stabilise, although this is normally followed by a decline into the dying phase over the next few days or weeks. This situation happens in less than 3 per cent of patients who are diagnosed as dying.

Initial assessment The initial assessment includes five sections, such as comfort measures, communication and psychological support, and 11 goals, from prescription of subcutaneous drugs to identifying the religious and spiritual needs of the family. The goals contained in the pathway outline the key outcomes of care, and incorporate nationally-agreed guidelines and research-based evidence whenever possible. Health care professionals are prompted by these goals and record whether they have been achieved.

Ongoing assessment Once the initial assessment has been completed, control of key symptoms, including pain, agitation, nausea and vomiting and respiratory tract secretions, is recorded as achieved or not achieved.

Four-hourly observations are made regarding symptom control, comfort measures, medication, treatments and procedures.

Twelve-hourly observations are recorded regarding mobility, safety, psychological insight and religious support.

Care of the relatives after death This section has goals related to the care and support of the patient's family and others, immediately after death. It also includes special needs in relation to the patient's body after death and what information should be given to the family. This includes information related to legal duties and a bereavement leaflet. This section of the pathway is completed by the ward staff and also by the staff in the General Office in the hospital.

Supporting documentation In order to successfully implement the LCP, a number of supporting documents need to be available to inform the health care professionals. There also needs to be the following supporting literature available to relatives –

- guidelines for symptom control
- information to carers including resources and facilities available in the hospital
- an information leaflet regarding the changes the relatives can expect in the dying phase
- bereavement leaflet.

The poor quality of care for dying patients was recognised in the National Cancer Plan, 2000. In the Cancer Plan, the challenge was given to raise the care of the dying to the level of the best. Since that time, the LCP has been disseminated widely to over 100 centres across the United Kingdom, all of which are actively involved in work related to the LCP and its implementation. The LCP has successfully been put into practice not just in hospitals but also in the community and nursing home sectors. The End of Life Initiative by the Department of Health is currently facilitating the dissemination of the LCP. The LCP Framework has the potential to promote care of the dying as a quality indicator in hospitals. This would promote the dissemination of best practice for care of the dying as developed in hospices so that it was delivered by health care professionals in hospitals. The result would be a good death for all.

NHS End of Life Care Programme

The aim of the programme is to provide sensitive quality care for all dying patients, irrespective of disease, and in all settings (home, hospital, hospice and care homes), by enabling more people to have choices of care at the end of life. This programme is the first step towards improving end of life care for all. There is still a lot to be done.

Why do we need the End of Life Care Programme?

About 500,000 people die every year in England and 84 per cent of these are over the age of 65. A study undertaken by Professor Irene Higginson shows that 56 per cent of people would wish to die at home. Yet, currently, if your loved one has cancer, he or she would have a one in four likelihood of dying at home. If your loved one has a disease other than cancer, he or she would have a one in five likelihood of being cared for at home. An increasing number of people are dying in care homes but at present the majority dies in hospital.

Why do we not die in our place of choice? Health and social care professionals do not always find out what the individual and their carer's needs are and, as individuals, we may not think anyone can help so we do not tell the professional. The services we need may not be available; alternatively, we may not even be aware that these services exist. It may also be true that professionals themselves do not always know what is on offer, as information on the services available from health, social and voluntary organisations may not always be widely publicised. Communication of information (whether this is verbal, written or other) and coordination of services are always a challenge to providers, patients and their carers.

What are the proposed outcomes of the programme?

- To increase the opportunity for individuals and their carers to have greater choice in where they want to be cared for when they are coming to the end of their life.
- To decrease the number of individuals who are admitted to an acute hospital despite having expressed a wish to die at home.
- To reduce the number of individuals who are transferred from a care home to an acute hospital in the last week of life.
- To educate doctors, nurses, social workers and other health and social care staff in understanding the needs of people at the end of life by ensuring better coordination, by sharing information and by supporting individuals and their carers in order that they can maintain control at a very stressful time.

How will this be achieved?

By providing doctors, nurses, social care and other health care staff with practical solutions on how they can improve end of life care for all. These have been put into three approaches.

1 The Gold Standards Framework This was developed by a group of doctors, nurses and users. It aims to improve the quality and organisation of end of life care provided by the whole primary care team (such as the patient's GP) and to provide better coworking with specialists. This framework is divided into seven key tasks, which focus on –

1 Communication.
2 Coordination of care.
3 Control of symptom control.
4 Continuity, including out-of-hours medical care and advanced care planning.
5 Continued learning for health and social care staff.
6 Carer support.
7 Care in the dying phase.

For more information via the relevant website, see Useful Information on pp.188–89.

2 The Liverpool Care Pathway for the Dying Patient (LCP) This was developed to take the best of hospice care and apply it to the care of people in hospital and in other settings including care homes (see pp.95–7). See Useful Information on pp.188–89.

3 The Preferred Place of Care Plan (PPC) This is a document that patients hold for themselves and take with them if they receive care in different places. It has space for patients' thoughts about their care and the choices they would like to make, including saying where they would want to be when they eventually die. Information about the family can also be recorded so that any new care staff can read about who's who and what matters to them too. If anything changes, this can be written in the plan so that it stays up to date. It is never too early to start a PPC plan. For the relevant website, see pp.188–89.

How can these three approaches help a dying person?

The combination of these approaches will enable those nearing the end of life to be identified and recorded in a register that will be kept at the GP practice so that doctors, nurses and others that may be involved in their care will be able to support them and their carer during this stage of their life.

In most cases, the next step would be that a nurse would either visit or contact patients via telephone to assess their own and their carer's needs. A plan of care would then be put together and agreed upon by all concerned, though another assessment might be required before this is possible.

During the initial or subsequent assessment it is important that the patient and carer ask the nurse, doctor or social worker about anything that might be worrying them. Also, when the patient and carer feel able to, it is important that they talk to the doctor, nurse or social worker about what the patient would like in terms of his or her end-of-life care –

- Do they want to be at home, if that is possible? The professionals will provide support and care but will not be able to provide 24-hour cover.
- Do they want to die in hospital? They may be very familiar with the staff and feel that this would be the best place for them.
- Would they prefer to be somewhere else, such as a hospice, a local community hospital or a care home.

These options need to be discussed with the doctor or nurse. However, it does not matter if the patient and/or carer do not remember to ask everything at the assessment; they should just make sure that they have a contact number so that they can ring up or arrange for the doctor or nurse to call again.

Other things that patient and carer may need to ask and which could be included in the assessment are –

- entitlement to benefits
- a disability badge for the car
- equipment, such as rails for the stairs
- other practical issues, such as finding someone to walk their dog
- how to deal with emergencies: either what the patient or carer could do or what number to ring
- information on local services, support groups, and what to expect
- symptom control, such as pain
- emotional support
- spiritual support
- carer support
- bereavement support.

The nurse, doctor or social worker that has undertaken the assessment will not be able to do everything themselves, so they may ask other people to come in to help or give advice. It is very important to make sure that the information is recorded. This can be done in a patient-held record, which they keep at all times. The patient and carer can both write in this and share information with doctors, nurses and other people who are caring for the dying person.

Another important point to remember is that doctors should share the information on the patient's condition and care with the out-of-hours doctor, so that if there is a problem during the night, the latter will know what has been happening and what the plan of care is.

Place of death: the options

Some people may feel uncomfortable about discussing where someone would prefer to be when they die. This is largely because it has a finite feel to it. If they are talking about place of death, it means they are definitely going to die. It all becomes a bit too real. Often these fears are held more by loved ones than the dying person him- or herself. Many patients feel glad to be given the opportunity to discuss things and make their wishes known. Once again it's all about control, about having the opportunity to direct the future in some small way. Some people may already have fixed views on where they do or don't want to be when they die. If someone has a clear view, it is still worth exploring the reasons for their wishes, as they may reflect underlying worries about something else.

"When my husband was in hospital, he was adamant that he did not want to die at home. I couldn't understand why. I thought he would want to be around his own things. When we spoke with him about it, it turned out that he just didn't want to be a burden to any of us. He was worried it would be too much for me to cope with."

The example above illustrates how we sometimes make decisions based on our concern for others. As it happened, this patient went home with extra support and assistance for his carers, so he was able to die in his own environment.

Whilst some people have clear views of where they want to be when they die, some do not. There are a few options available and it is worth looking at each one in turn because they each have their advantages and disadvantages.

Hospital

One hundred years ago, most people who died in the United Kingdom, died at home. These days, the majority of the population die in hospital. There are several reasons for this, and understanding why this has come about will enable you to see why different people end up in different places.

Advancing medical expertise

One hundred years ago, the management of a heart attack would be bed rest. There would be no need to admit a patient to hospital because the care they received there would be no different from that they would get at home. They either got better or they died. Now medicine has advanced so much that people with a suspected heart attack are rushed into hospital straight away. They might be given "clot busting drugs" to stop the heart attack or have their coronary arteries re-opened with angioplasty. There are a host of different medicines that can be given to stabilise the heart and prevent fatal heart rhythm abnormalities. Some people still die of heart attacks but many more can be treated and, as a result, the number of deaths has fallen significantly over the years. In the same way that more can be done for victims of heart attacks by sending them to hospital, we sometimes think that more can be done to make someone better even though they appear to be dying.

"I knew Dad was dying but I just wondered whether there was anything else that could be done for his chest. I dialled 999 too because I didn't want to feel I had done nothing."

As medicine advances, so people's expectations increase. What was viewed as a hopeless situation ten years ago may now be treatable. Unless you "err on the side of caution" and admit someone to hospital, you will never know. The sad fact remains that, all too often, people are admitted to hospital as an emergency when there is nothing further that can be done. The loved one needs to be kept comfortable and to receive tender loving care. Sometimes hospital is the appropriate place for this, whilst at other times it is not.

As medicine advances, so people's expectations increase. What was viewed as a hopeless situation ten years ago may now be treatable.

Loss of immediate extended family unit

On some occasions, people express a desire to die at home, but this is not possible because there is inadequate support available. One hundred years ago, the average family unit remained in the same geographical area. The children and grandchildren lived a few doors down the road. Other relations lived nearby. If someone was ill, the whole family was available to help out and take turns. Nowadays, the average family unit is different. More often than not, families live further apart. As children get older, they move out of the area. When a loved one is unwell, families still try to drop everything to be with them, but it is harder to be on site all the time. When a person's support network is not nearby, it can be more challenging for them to be looked after at home, especially if they normally live alone.

Changing attitudes to death

Death is a normal part of life. From the day we are born, we are destined to die some day. A century ago, death was more common and we behaved differently towards it. For example, it was more common to have an open coffin in the living room for the neighbours to come and pay their respects. Nowadays, many of us are less comfortable with this. Some people do not wish to die at home because they worry their family will find this distressing.

The pros and cons of dying in hospital

Wherever one dies, there will be good points and bad points about each option. It is essential to recognise that these points are gross generalisations and not specific to any institution in particular. It is not possible to make an important decision about where a loved one might want to die on the basis of this book. The aim in the following pages is to highlight the things that people might want to consider and be aware of at a time when making clear decisions is often difficult.

Admission Getting in to hospital is almost always achievable and more people with terminal illness die in hospital than anywhere else. The only down side to this is that most hospitals admit patients through the same system: either via Accident and Emergency or via the Admissions Unit. If you have ever been admitted to hospital, you may have experienced a wait to be seen and to be given a bed. You will have seen the extremely busy staff running around as more people are admitted to hospital. The reality is that, sometimes, people who are admitted to hospital for terminal care pass away before they are admitted onto a ward. The nurses and doctors always do their best to allow a dying patient and their family to be in a private, peaceful environment, but this is sometimes not available in what is the busiest part of the hospital. The worst case scenario is when someone dies on a trolley in Accident and Emergency whilst waiting for a bed on a ward.

Environment Most hospitals are what we call District General Hospitals or DGHs. They look after a wide spectrum of medical and surgical conditions. They never close, and ward beds are rarely empty for long. They tend to be busy places and some people find they need to get home for a rest because the "busyness" of the wards keeps them awake.

Medical/Nursing cover The wards are always staffed with nurses, and doctors are present between 9 a.m. and 5 p.m. At night, the doctors are on call to cover the wards. This means that they may not be on the ward, but can be bleeped by the nurses if they are needed. They remain within the hospital during the on-call period.

Equipment Hospitals have got it all: a pharmacy full of medicines, machines and x-ray facilities in the same building, and blood test laboratories on site. In short, all that a patient needs can be catered for in the hospital. It is important to remember, though, that a dying patient may not need things like blood tests and x-rays.

Expertise DGHs are general hospitals and, although all doctors and nurses there have experience of looking after dying patients, it is rarely the main focus of their skills or training. Hospital staff focus more on treating illness and offering cures. Sometimes this is less appropriate for someone who is dying. They don't need drips, antibiotics and tests; they need to be made comfortable, to maintain their dignity, and to be looked after with compassion. Most hospitals have a palliative care team, which usually consists of specialist palliative care nurses and sometimes a palliative care doctor. They are available to offer advice to the teams looking after dying patients.

Resuscitation Hospitals have resuscitation equipment and a suitably trained resuscitation team who will try to restart someone's heart if they have a cardiac arrest. All hospitals have a resuscitation policy to help them decide when and when not to attempt resuscitation. This issue is covered in more detail in Chapter 6.

Support Hospitals have a chaplaincy service and hospital visitors who are available to talk with families. Staff are also available to offer emotional support, but often they are very busy with the basics of care, and they do not always have the opportunity to support patients as much as they would like. This is often a cause of sadness for many nurses who wish their jobs allowed them more time to give emotional support to patients and their carers.

Visiting There are usually visiting restrictions but these are often flexible for families of dying patients (*see Chapter 2*).

Communication issues in hospital

The telephone When someone is in hospital, no matter how well or unwell they are, it can sometimes be difficult to get useful information on their condition, particularly over the phone. Health care professionals are not allowed to reveal any details of a patient's diagnosis, treatment, condition or prognosis unless they have the clear permission of the patient in question. Even if permission has been granted, the professionals still need to know that you are who you say you are, and that is impossible over the phone.

All patients have the right to confidentiality and to decide who has access to knowledge of their condition. For that reason, you are unlikely to get much useful information over the phone, other than news of how they slept or what they had for breakfast. This can be frustrating if you are calling from far away and need to know whether to fly over to see the dying person. Often the best thing to do is to leave a contact number with the ward, asking for one of the medical team to contact you for an update. This can be a useful way of getting information, assuming the patient is happy for you to be given details of his or her condition. If there are other friends or family visiting, it is usually better to get updates from them. Whilst medical and nursing staff try to keep friends and family updated, this is much easier to do if the information is given via an agreed key family member who takes responsibility to keep everyone else informed (*see p.93*).

When someone is admitted to hospital, they are asked to identify a next-of-kin. This is particularly important when the person is dying, since important conversations may need to occur with that person. At this point, the admitting staff (usually a nurse) will ask for the next-of-kin's contact details. In addition, they will ask whether they would want to be contacted if there is any change. What they are really asking is this:

"If your loved one becomes more unwell or we think that they may be imminently dying, do you want us to call you even if it is the middle of the night?"

This is the time that you need to be explicit about what you want. If you want to be called in to be with the person when he or she is dying, say so. If you only want to be contacted when the person has passed away, you can say that as well.

Face-to-face contact It is often best to get information face to face when you visit the patient. Who you talk to will be determined by the following –

1 Who you have access to on the ward.
2 What level of information you are looking for.

The most accessible health care professionals on the ward are the nursing staff. They will be the ones who spend the most time with the patient and will have the most up-to-date information about his or her general wellbeing and progress. The level of information available from members of the nursing team varies between hospitals, and largely depends on the way the team works and interacts with the doctors. It is not enough that someone can tell you about the patient's condition, they also need to be able to answer questions arising from this. Sometimes members of the nursing team will suggest you talk to one of the doctors so you can get all the information you need.

If you ask to speak with one of the doctors, you are most likely to see one of the more junior members of the team, called House Officers and Senior House Officers. House Officers (HOs) are newly qualified doctors, who have graduated from medical school in the past year. They work closely with Senior House Officers (SHOs) who have a few more years' experience. They are the doctors who will see your loved one daily. They are often on the wards and reasonably easy to get hold of (via the nurses). Nonetheless, they are very busy and it is worth picking a key family member to be involved in all communications, to avoid repetition. They are able to answer most questions that you would have, although it is always better to arrange a time to speak with them so they can plan their schedule accordingly.

... it is worth picking a key family member to be involved in all communications ...

Occasionally, the House Officer or SHO will be unable to give you the information you need. You may need to speak with a more senior member of the team such as the Specialist Registrar (SpR). They are doctors who have done all their postgraduate exams and have gained enough experience that they are working towards being a consultant. They often have other commitments than just the wards and will be in different places around the hospital. If you need to speak with the SpR, the SHO may need to contact them. Alternatively, an appointment can be made via the nurses.

The Consultant is the head of the team and takes ultimate responsibility for the care of the patients. Your loved one may know the Consultant already. Often people are under the same Consultant for years as an outpatient. They may forge a strong relationship with the Consultant and this becomes apparent as a patient nears the end of life. Consultants tend to have other roles beyond clinical patient care. They may be in meetings, teaching at university, or in operating theatres. The days of Consultants spending half their lives on the golf course are now well and truly over. They might be difficult to track down on occasion, but are almost always contactable via their secretary. There may be times when the only one who can answer your questions is the Consultant. If this is the case, there are two options –

1 Request an appointment with the Consultant (via the ward or their secretary).

2 Ask to be present on the next Consultant ward round: this is not always possible for many clinical reasons but you could suggest this to the ward team. Whatever you do, do not just turn up.

Pros and cons when dealing with different doctors

Grade of doctor	What this means	Pros of seeing them	Cons of seeing them
House Officer (HO)	Junior member of team. Qualified less than a year.	Easy to get hold of. On the wards most of the time.	May not have all the answers.
Senior House Officer (SHO)	Qualified 1–4 years but still a junior team member.	On the wards most of the time but not as much as HO.	Will have more information than HO.
Specialist Registrar (SpR)	Experienced. Training to be a consultant.	Should be able to answer most questions.	Very busy. Harder to get hold of than HO/ SHO.
Consultant	The boss. Responsible for the patient.	Most experienced. Has most answers.	Will need an appointment.

Important questions   There are some things that doctors might not tell you unless they are asked directly. This can be for several reasons –

1 They don't have the answer.

2 They don't want to upset you with bad news.

3 They haven't considered this is something you want to know.

If you don't ask the question, you won't get the answer and sometimes you need to get the answer clarified so that you can understand it. For example, you may ask something like –

"Is he dying?"

A straightforward question really, but not always greeted with a straightforward answer.

The responses I have heard include:

"Of course not! He'll be fine!" which means, *"I wish you hadn't asked me that. I always feel awkward telling people their loved one is dying. How about if I just pretend it's all OK, so we all feel better for a while?"*

"Well he's not dying dying," which means, *"Yup, he's dying but I'm not sure when."*

"Well none of us can predict the future," which means, *"Look I can't predict the future but I know enough about patients to tell you that things are bad. I'm just not comfortable telling you this because you might cry."*

If you get a response like this, it is sometimes useful to clarify what you need to know and explain to the doctor why you need this information. In this way, you are giving them permission to give you bad news. It's as if you are saying, "Look, I know this is difficult but I need you to tell me if he is dying. I'm prepared to accept the truth."

I can't give you a script of what you should say. Each situation is different but the following lines may be useful for you to consider or adapt if you need to use them.

"He is looking more unwell to me. I know that this isn't curable. Do you think he is dying now?"

"I know it's difficult to be sure about these things, but there are people I need to inform, should he take a turn for the worse."

One word of warning: do not ask a question if you are not prepared to hear the answer. Some doctors may give a straight answer to a question because they believe that is what you want. Doctors try to "read" the people they are talking to for clues on how best to speak with them. Do they want straight talking or are they vulnerable and need to be told gently?

Another difficult question to get a straight answer to is:

"How long does he have to live?"

The reason this won't get a straight answer is because no one really knows for sure. The best doctors can give you is an educated guess based on their knowledge and experience. Any doctor who predicts a specific time is giving you their best guess, nothing more.

Once again, I think it is important to clarify why you need this information. Sometimes doctors can at least give you a ball park figure to help guide you with any plans you might have. For example, if someone is told their cancer is incurable, they may want to know their life expectancy, not so they can tick days off on the calendar, but so they can decide whether they can take one last trip to Paris while they are well enough. A prognosis in terms of years, months, weeks, days or hours might be useful then.

In the hospital setting, knowing whether the dying person is likely to be alive for hours or days will help a family to decide whether they should stay overnight, whether other relatives should be called from around the country (and beyond) and how long they are likely to be off work for on compassionate leave. Saying something like the following can be useful when talking to health care professionals:

"I know it is impossible to predict, but there are some close relatives who live several hours' drive away. Do you think we need to be calling them down?"

"I understand that no one can be certain how long he has got before he dies. Do you think he is likely to die in the next few hours? Should I stay with him tonight?"

Hospice

You are probably familiar with your local hospice, you may even have raised money for it. However, it is worth dispelling a few myths about hospices:

- "They are just places where people go to die." Over 50 per cent of people admitted to hospices are discharged. This is because some people are admitted for symptom control such as pain or sickness. Some people are admitted for care during the last days of life but many people are in-patients just for the time it takes to get their symptoms under control.
- "They are very religious places." The original hospices were founded by people of the Christian faith. Hospices recognise that people are of all faiths and that some people have no religious beliefs. They attempt to offer support to everyone, in keeping with each person's belief system.
- "It costs money to go there." Hospice admission is free of charge to patients. It doesn't cost them a penny. Hospices are primarily funded by charitable donations and in part by the NHS.

Admission Hospices have limited bed numbers and so it is not always possible for people to get in when they need to. There is often a waiting list, and sometimes people waiting to get in will end up being looked after at home or in hospital. The other issue with hospices is that they were originally designed to look after cancer patients with less emphasis on the needs of non-cancer patients. Although the palliative care needs of non-cancer patients are being increasingly recognised, hospices still provide an in-patient service predominantly to patients with cancer.

Environment Hospices are lovely places. Almost all patients who go there rave about them. They tend to be very calm and peaceful, and although they look after many people with terminal disease, they tend to be very happy places. They are less busy than hospitals and people will be admitted directly onto the ward; there is no waiting in A&E.

Medical/Nursing cover The doctors and nurses are specialists at delivering palliative care. They are highly skilled at managing complex symptoms and communicating with families and patients. The ratio of nurses to patients is higher than in hospital, so there is more nursing time per patient. There will be nursing cover at all times and doctors present during the day. At night, the doctor will be on call but not resident in the hospice.

Equipment Hospices are fully equipped with all that is needed to deliver palliative care. However, they do not have some of the high-tech machines that you would find in hospital. If patients need an x-ray, for example, they may need to go to hospital to have one done. Much of the patient care is based on clinical examination and assessment.

Expertise Hospices can provide care for patients with advanced terminal illness and manage end of life emergencies. They cannot offer all the active interventions and general medical expertise found in a hospital.

Resuscitation In the same way that most hospitals have a resuscitation policy, so do hospices. However, they usually state that they will not offer cardiopulmonary resuscitation (CPR) to a patient if they arrest. The issues surrounding resuscitation in a hospice are beyond the scope of this chapter, but it is worth being aware that hospices are unlikely to perform CPR on patients. In truth, if someone is admitted to a hospice to die, CPR would be futile and inappropriate in almost all situations.

Support The staff tend to be highly specialised in recognising the emotional needs not only of the patient, but also of the family. Nursing and medical staff are more available for discussions about prognosis and are trained specifically to discuss difficult situations. Hospices often have a specialist palliative care social worker who can help with financial difficulties and home worries. There is often a bereavement service available for families when their loved one has died.

Visiting Hospices have an open visiting policy, although they may request that visitors respect a two-hour quiet period so the patients can rest in the middle of the day.

Communication issues within hospices By and large, this is handled well in hospices. There are several reasons why this is so –

- Good communication skills. Both doctors and nurses in hospices are highly skilled in communicating with dying patients and their families. They have often been on training courses to develop their communication skills.
- The staff have time. This may sound very basic, but a doctor or nurse who is rushing around is less likely to have the time to discuss a difficult situation with you. The staffing levels in a hospice are such that "talking time" is built into the daily schedule. Staff expect to communicate regularly with patients and key family members.
- Multiprofessional working. Hospital teams tend to be quite hierarchical, with the doctors making all the decisions and the nurses following these plans. For some specialties, this is an appropriate model of care. In the care of the dying, a better system of working recognises the greater importance of professionals, other than just the doctor, directing care. Patient care will be decided from input by nurses, physiotherapists, pharmacists, occupational therapists, chaplains and doctors, to name but a few. In the same way, communication with the family will not lie solely with the doctors. The nursing staff will be just as able to discuss the situation with the family and patient.

Communication in hospices is done well. But to give a little balance to the picture, it is worth being aware of some potential pitfalls. When a team is so readily available to discuss things with you, it is important not to lose sight of the patient. It can be tempting to have conversation after conversation with the family, without involving the patient.

Another issue for hospice teams is to get the balance right when talking to patients. Yes, they can talk about sad things with a patient. Yes, they can have deep and meaningful conversations daily if needed, but they need to ensure that this is what the patient wants and needs.

As mentioned in the previous chapter, a terminal disease does not define a person. The person has been on this planet for many years prior to getting ill. People don't want heavy conversations all the time. Sometimes they just need a normal chat, knowing that if they have something difficult to ask, they can. Equally, even if they are in a hospice, some patients remain in denial about their situation until their death – or at least choose not to talk about it, as is their right. It is important to be comfortable with discussing death and dying, but remember that these discussions are not required all the time.

Dying at home

A man's home is his castle, and it doesn't sound too much to ask for to be able to die in one's own home, surrounded by one's own family. The truth is that dying in hospital, although not ideal for most people, is the easiest option when someone with a terminal illness becomes more unwell. If a GP is called to the home of someone who is dying, their first thought will be to admit them to hospital (or the hospice if there is a bed). It is rare for someone to remain at home to die unless those wishes have been specifically made and planned for previously.

Admission There is no waiting list and no Admissions Unit. You are there already. The challenge is staying there and ensuring that you have adequate back-up and support to help you remain there, even when things take a turn for the worse.

Environment Hospitals and hospices run to certain rules. Breakfast will be served at a particular time followed by the medicine round at a specific time later. As nice as these places are, they can be a bit too regimented, too institutionalised. If you're in your own home, you can do what you want, when you want. There are no patients disturbing you, no doctors wandering in at all hours, no noise keeping you awake at night. Being in your own environment is comfort enough.

If you're in your own home, you can do what you want, when you want.

It is important to remember certain things will change as a loved one gets more unwell. Many daily activities that we take for granted can become almost impossible as someone becomes weaker and more disabled by terminal illness. In short we need to acknowledge that a home that was perfect for a well person may be a struggle when he or she is ill. When considering dying at home, we need to be prepared to make some compromises to ensure this is not only feasible, but also safe. Compromises include where to have the bed and which toilet to use? It may be easier to have the bed downstairs, and if the toilet is too far away, would a bottle or a commode be acceptable?

Medical/Nursing cover One of the major issues about dying at home is that there is unlikely to be round-the-clock nursing care; if all dying patients at home had a nurse 24 hours a day, more people would be able to die in their own environment. Sadly, many patients who want to die at home end up being admitted to hospital when things don't work out. If someone wishes to remain at home to die, the following services are available (these may vary from region to region according to local health care funding and provision):

1 **District Nurses.** These highly qualified and skilled community nurses can make regular visits to assess the patient, provide nursing care and work with other team members to provide symptom control. They operate an on-call service and input is often increased as someone becomes more unwell.

2 **Night Sitters.** These are usually nursing auxiliaries who are present at night to help care for the patient. They are not qualified to administer drugs, but they are there to provide some respite for family members and allow them to have some sleep.

3 **Specialist Palliative Care Nurses.** These nurses are highly specialised in providing symptom control advice to the community team. They are usually affiliated to a local palliative care service and work with the support of a palliative care consultant. Their role is usually advisory and they are not involved in the hands-on nursing duties.

4 **Hospice at Home.** Some regions provide a Hospice at Home or Rapid Response service, providing significant hands-on nursing care for the last few days of life. Unfortunately, the availability varies across Britain and this model is not yet standard for all.

5 **General Practitioner.** Good GPs will do their utmost to help one of their patients remain at home if it is their wish. There are a great many outstanding GPs who go to enormous lengths to do what is right for their patients and look after them at home.

Although there are many professionals working hard to ensure someone who wants to die at home, it must be stressed that in most situations, round-the-clock nursing care is not provided and there will be times when family members are alone with the loved one. There is still someone on the end of a phone, someone on call, but they will not be there at the touch of a button, like in hospital. In the same way, if someone needed an injection for pain or sickness, the district nurse would need to come in to do it. Some families prefer it this way. They see it as their role, their loving duty to care for their loved one. Some even find it intrusive to have strangers coming into their home to help. Most people, though, value the input and support from the community team and hope for more, rather than less.

Equipment Obviously a person's home is not equipped with all the high-tech features of a hospital. Nevertheless, specialist equipment needed to care for the dying at home can be provided by the district nursing service. For example, when people become unwell, they move around less and become prone to bed sores. There are special mattresses to help this. Also, nursing a patient on a conventional bed can be difficult for a host of reasons. Patients can be better cared for on hospital-style beds, which can be provided in the community. Occupational therapists may visit the home to assess if there are any aids or appliances that can make the patient's stay at home easier. Simple things like a commode or shower stool may make the world of difference.

Expertise By and large, the expertise provided in the community for the dying patient is very good. Obviously this varies from region to region, but the teams aim to care for their patients in the community and provide, for want of a better word, "good old-fashioned nursing care". Community patients have the support of a specialist palliative care nurse who works closely with the district nurses and the GP, backed up by the advice and support of a local palliative medicine doctor.

Resuscitation If someone has chosen to remain at home to die, it is important to acknowledge that the resuscitation facilities are the same as for anyone at home: non-existent. If someone arrests, you dial 999. In the case of someone with a terminal illness who is dying, calling 999 to resuscitate them seems counter-intuitive to what we are trying to achieve. Chapter 6 covers the issues around resuscitation in more detail.

Support People at home have the support of their General Practice and the community palliative care team. The district nurses are highly skilled in supporting loved ones and the specialist palliative care nurse will also be skilled in counselling. Any patient and family known to the palliative care service should be able to access the bereavement services if the General Practice does not offer one.

The district nurses are highly skilled in supporting loved ones and the specialist palliative care nurse will also be skilled in counselling.

Visiting This is an entirely personal matter. Some people welcome lots of visitors, whilst others find it intrusive. At least in hospital it is possible to put a limit on visitors. This is harder at home.

Points to consider

Below is a table covering the main points that need to be considered when planning a place of death. Not all the points are applicable for each person and there are many other things you may want to think about.

	Hospital	Hospice	Home
Admission	Anyone can be admitted. May need to go via Casualty or Admissions Ward.	Limited availability. Often a waiting list.	Always there. May need to compromise.
Environment	Noisy, busy institution.	Quiet, gorgeous. Like hotels.	It's home.
Medical/ Nursing cover	Nurses present all the time, doctors resident on call. Nursing ratios less.	Nursing all the time, doctors on call but not resident. Higher ratio of nurses.	Strong reliance on family input. GP, district nurses.
Expertise	Generalist, curative focus. Hospital Palliative Care team.	Specialist holistic care. Not emergency providers.	General holistic care. Experience of caring for the dying.
Equipment	Got it all.	May need to travel for tests like x-rays.	Community will bring in equipment that is needed.
Resuscitation	Available.	Not available.	Not available.
Support	Chaplaincy. All nurses have experience.	Lots and lots.	Family, district nurse, GP, community.
Visiting	Restricted but flexible when dying.	Open.	Up to you.

Support for carers

In order for carers to be able to care for a dying person, they need to be able to look after themselves too. All too often, carers tire themselves out quickly. If their loved one is in hospital, they spend all their time travelling back and forth to visit. In addition, they try to balance the other parts of their lives such as looking after the children or going to work. Add to this the emotional energy involved in coming to terms with a loved one's illness and it is easy to see why people can quickly arrive at the brink of a nervous breakdown. When a dying person is at home, the pressures can be even greater. Many patients re-admitted to hospital, having been discharged home to die, often return because the family have been unable to cope and not because the patient's condition has worsened. As carers, you must recognise certain facts of life.

You have not been trained for this

Coping with the impending death of someone you care for is a truly awful experience and there are no rules about how you should cope. No one expects you to have the skills of a trained doctor or nurse. All one can expect is the love and compassion that you are exhibiting in abundance by acting as a carer for your loved one. It is also worth remembering, as mentioned earlier, that nurses have scheduled breaks at work. However, families are there, 24 hours a day, without formal breaks. If external help is offered to you, take it.

You are not superhuman

John Diamond's experience of cancer is brilliantly recorded in his book, *C: Because Cowards Get Cancer Too*. What makes this book so helpful for others is the fact that he makes no pretence of being brave or a "coper". He talks about being scared about the cancer journey. We often read about people's bravery as they "fight their battle with cancer" or about how wonderful a family member was in caring for someone during their illness. It makes it all scarier really because it raises expectations of how we, as carers, are supposed to manage. The reality is that you are not superhuman; you are not expected to handle more than you can cope with.

No one is judging you

No one can effectively judge you because they do not know you or what you are going through. It is normal to worry about what other people think of us, but that is their problem.

Most people are just concerned and want to make sure you have enough help. You must do what you need to do to get through this.

Some hints on how to cope

The most important advice for a carer is this: what you are going through is difficult and it is likely you will need help in one way or another.

Recognising this inevitability will help you to keep an eye on your own coping levels and to get help if you start to get overwhelmed by the situation. Below are a few other hints on how to cope. They are not in any particular order and not all may be useful for you. Focus on the ones that seem to help you the most:

Recognise that one person cannot do it alone When your loved one was cared for in hospital, there was a whole team of professionals involved in looking after him or her. These people are specially trained to look after the sick and dying. It doesn't make sense that one untrained person can manage all this alone. There is only one of you, and you will need other people to help you at some stage. As well as seeking help from health care teams, you might also need to ask friends to do some shopping for you, or ask them to look after the children for a while. Don't be too proud to ask.

Have at least one afternoon a week to yourself This is easier said than done, but try to have one afternoon a week to yourself. Time to be you, not a carer, nor a loved one. It cannot be stressed enough how important this is. By having your own space, albeit for a short time, you will help maintain the strength to carry on. People do not suddenly find it hard to cope. It is something that creeps up on them. It is the relentless nature of being a carer with no respite. Ask your GP or Clinical Nurse Specialist whether there are day sitters available who could spend half a day at home whilst you go out for a while.

By having your own space, albeit for a short time, you will help maintain the strength to carry on.

Have someone you can talk to When someone is dying, it can seem that everyone is offering support to the patient, but no one is considering your needs. Yet it is normal to want to talk to someone about your own worries. This is not selfish behaviour; this is sensible if you are to remain physically and psychologically strong for the dying person you are caring for. If you have a close friend you can talk to, use him or her. If not, ask your GP about seeking professional help. Do not be afraid to talk openly about your own feelings and worries. Sometimes we can lose perspective on how we are doing, the thoughts we are having and our ability to manage. It will help if you can unburden yourself to someone trustworthy.

Eat healthily and regularly We often forget to take care of ourselves when we focus on caring for a dying person. Try to avoid eating nutritionally poor foods. Imagine that you are like a wall that needs to be strong because of the support you want to offer your loved one. If you start depriving yourself of healthy food, you will start to weaken the wall. You don't want to get to the stage where the wall collapses. Takeaway foods are convenient but not a long-term answer. Try not to skip meals either; it's much better to get yourself into a routine that works. And although a beer or glass of wine are nice ways to relax at the end of the day, if you find yourself drinking in order to cope, seek help.

Exercise No one is suggesting that because your loved one is dying you should join a gym and get fit. However, regular exercise is good for us and that applies even when caring for a dying person. Going for a walk or a run can help you to relax, clear your head and keep your body healthy.

Do not pretend you are fine if you are not Often, we can see clearly when someone else is struggling, but are unable to recognise the signs when the situation relates to us. If you think you are going under, you probably are. If someone asks, be honest. Do not suffer in silence. People can only help you (and they will) if they know you need help.

Stay in close touch with your GP GPs should be made aware that you are caring for someone who is dying. They will want to know how you are managing and whether there is anything they or their team can do to help. Stay in close touch with them so that they can do their job, which is to look after you.

Are you entitled to financial assistance? When someone is dying, there are various benefits to which the patient and the carers are entitled. Financial worries often dominate carers and the patient, especially if they have had to put work on hold for a while. Find out whether you are entitled to any benefits. Ask your GP or Clinical Nurse Specialist to put you in touch with someone who can help with this.

Euthanasia/Physician-assisted suicide

Some people who have a terminal illness will think about death and dying a lot. On occasion, they may request something called euthanasia. People's opinions about euthanasia are divided and they tend to feel passionately about it, whether they are for or against it. Rather than provide a blow-by-blow account of the euthanasia debate, it might be more useful to answer a few of the more common questions that are asked on the subject.

What is the difference between euthanasia and physician-assisted suicide?

The word euthanasia is derived from the Greek words "eu" and "thanatos", which together mean "good death". The Voluntary Euthanasia Society defines euthanasia as "a good death brought about by a doctor providing drugs to bring a peaceful end to the dying process". In practical terms this means that if someone with a terminal illness asks for euthanasia, they are asking their doctor to administer them medicines that will end their life.

Physician-assisted suicide (PAS) is when someone asks the doctor to provide them with the medicines that will shorten their life. In this situation, patients kill themselves, but using medicines that the doctor has prescribed.

The word euthanasia is derived from the Greek words "eu" and "thanatos" which together mean "good death".

Why do people request euthanasia or PAS?

There are many reasons why people may request euthanasia or PAS. Some people see euthanasia as a matter of their personal freedom and something that they have a right to request. People may view it as a way of avoiding future psychological or physical suffering or a way out of the distress they are currently experiencing. When patients ask a doctor to help end their life, they do so because they fear the future and fear how their illness will progress. They also feel so out of control of their own lives that they at least want to exert some control over when and how they die. Some patients also worry about being a burden to their carers and feel that they would be better off dead rather than put loved ones through the pain of having to look after them.

What are the arguments for euthanasia/PAS?

The pro-euthanasia campaigners see it as a matter of personal freedom. Since suicide is no longer illegal in the United Kingdom, they argue that an essential part of civilised society is that people can be helped to die pain free and with dignity. They argue that failing to help someone end their life is immoral and that, for example, a failed suicide may cause even more distress. To many, euthanasia seems a way of avoiding suffering and distress.

What are the arguments against euthanasia/PAS?

From a religious perspective, life is sacrosanct and only God can decide when to end it. Euthanasia and PAS are immoral and a sin. Clearly we live in a society where only a proportion of people have religious beliefs and so this argument may only be of relevance to those of religious faith.

Some would suggest that those who request euthanasia/PAS on the grounds of physical or emotional suffering do so without having access to specialist palliative care. Indeed, it regularly happens that patients request euthanasia as a way to end their unbearable pain and no longer do so once they have their pain effectively managed by the palliative care services. Likewise, some patients make such requests at a time when they are profoundly depressed. Once their depression has been managed and appropriate support given, they no longer feel the need to request euthanasia.

… patients request euthanasia as a way to end their unbearable pain and no longer do so once they have their pain effectively managed by the palliative care services.

Another concern of those against euthanasia/PAS is that it will put vulnerable adults at risk. Those who do not want to be a burden, those who require extensive support and expertise, and those under pressure from families unwilling to look after them, may request euthanasia as an easier option.

Do many patients ask for euthanasia/PAS?

The answer to this is not straightforward because talking about these issues does not necessarily mean someone wants euthanasia. A patient might say:

"I wish you could give me a pill to end it all," or *"I wish you could give me euthanasia."*

If a patient says something like this, the first thing to do is explore with them the reasons they have been thinking about euthanasia. Many are trying to verbalise their overall distress and are looking for an opportunity to raise issues that are bothering them. Sometimes they feel so out of control with the illness that the only thing they feel they can control is their death, if euthanasia is available. To some, it is almost a reassuring notion that if things get too bad, there are always other options.

Where does palliative care fit in with all this?

First and foremost, palliative care doctors did not train to be euthanasia doctors and most oppose euthanasia/PAS. I think it is important to note that a group of professionals who look after the dying and their families are of this opinion. Many palliative care teams believe that access to palliative care services for all people with terminal illness would lessen the demand for euthanasia. There are not enough palliative care services around the country at the moment and so it is difficult to know whether euthanasia PAS would be requested as much if we had the full quota of required palliative care professionals in position.

A cynic might say that legalised euthanasia is a cheaper option than providing necessary medical and support services for patients who may request a premature end to their life. Twenty-four hour care, psychological support and specialist back-up all cost money. Euthanasia is much cheaper.

What can I do as a carer?

We often hear deeply sad stories of relatives who are arrested and tried for the "mercy killing" of a loved one. I cannot imagine how much anguish carers must have felt if the only option for them was to kill someone to end their suffering. Often the relative is subjected to a full criminal investigation and court trial and given a suspended sentence or found not guilty of criminal charges. However, this does not take away the distress of the bereavement and the process of facing a trial. How did it get to this point? What supports were available to the patient and carer?

Your role as a carer is to support your loved one through his or her illness and at times to be his or her advocate. If symptoms are not being addressed, push for a palliative care referral. Make sure that psychological support services are accessed. The bottom line is this: you should not be put in a position where ending the life of a suffering loved one is the only option. There are support services available. Make sure you are put in touch with them.

Chapter 4 Bereavement and mourning

Grief is a natural reaction to loss – and the loss of a person who has been a significant, perhaps the most significant, part of your life can be overwhelmingly painful. The range of emotions, almost all of them negative, can be shocking: anger, guilt, depression, fear and anxiety create a sense of being unsafe, at sea, empty of love. Understanding the process of bereavement will not prevent this pain. But it can help to chart a path back to some kind of normal life.

Although the process of bereavement is ultimately healing, loss and grief are not diseases where recovery is the ultimate goal. Rather, you embark on a process of adjusting to a different way of living: of carrying on without the person you have lost; of slowly beginning to look forwards more often than looking backwards; maybe, even, of gaining wisdom and insight that can help both you and others.

There are no rules

Perhaps the most important lesson from those who have gone through bereavement and been able to talk about the experience is that there are no rules on how to proceed. "One person wants to be private, another to shout from the rooftops; one finds physical comfort and loads of hugs and kisses a comfort, others shrink away, hiding like a wounded animal," says agony aunt, Virginia Ironside in her book, *You'll Get Over It.*

Warmth and rest help almost everyone in the early days following the loss of a loved one. Thereafter, support from friends and relatives and sometimes counselling is likely to be invaluable, especially with the acknowledgement that we are as individual in bereavement as at other times.

Faiths and belief systems

"No society has found a satisfactory way of dealing with the death of a loved one", says bereavement expert, Dr Colin Murray-Parkes. But most try. Grief is individual but bereavement has become a ritual in most cultures. At a time of great vulnerability, it often helps people to be told what to do. It gives them something to latch on to at a time when they are most in turmoil.

Grief is individual but bereavement has become a ritual in most cultures.

Burial or cremation?

As will be seen in the following chapter, there are many different ways of burying the dead. Burials are insisted on by those who belong to a religion that has a belief in resurrection: Judaism, Islam and Roman Catholicism. People whose faith revolves around reincarnation, including Hindus, Sikhs and Buddhists, almost always cremate their dead. As sociologist Dr Tony Walter points out, "The earthiness of burial seems to fit the physicality of the belief in bodily resurrection, while the dissipation of smoke into the air and of ashes into the river frees the soul to find another incarnation."

In Europe, cremation is almost unknown in Catholic countries, including Eire, Spain, France and Italy. In the latter, for example, less than 1 per cent of the deceased are cremated. Whereas in countries with a Protestant and often largely secular background, people are likely to opt for cremation.

It is frequently believed that the high rate of cremations in some countries is due to lack of space. But that's not true, says Dr Walter, pointing out that Canada and Australia have more cremations than Belgium and The Netherlands. In many countries, cremation is preferred because it is viewed as non-religious. "The relatively high use of cremation in Britain (70 per cent)," he says, "has got far more to do with the fact we are squeamish about re-using graves, unlike those practical Europeans who dig up the bones and start again … most frequently re-using graves on a 10–20 year cycle."

Within Christianity, funerals in Catholic countries remain an occasion for prayer for the salvation of the deceased's soul. In Protestant and Orthodox countries, funeral services are increasingly seen as support for the bereaved, giving them a chance to express and share their grief.

The cost of funerals

Extravagance is the norm in many countries, particularly those with large immigrant communities. In many parts of the US, the funeral remains the showy event described by Jessica Mitford's 1963 exposé, *The American Way of Death*. Thousands of dollars are spent on the embalmed, made-up body, which is dressed in expensive clothes and lies in a splendidly lined casket, destined to be buried in a cemetary that looks like a theme park. Not everyone approves.

"They put shoes on the dead that are comfortable to wear, with silk pillows to lie on, and rouge on the cheeks, so they look like they're only asleep. It's so phony and so dishonest," commented psychiatrist, American Elisabeth Kübler-Ross, one of the first to rethink the philosophy of dying.

The point of these extravaganzas, according to Mitford is that they necessitate some degree of sacrifice, thereby "permitting the survivors to atone for any real or fancied neglect prior to death". As a result, according to Dr Walter, "In 20th-century America, the funeral director grows fat through ordinary people paying him to deal with guilt and sin – as the priest did in late medieval Europe".

Alongside guilt, however, there is the sheer feel-good factor of spending on one's loved ones, with the level of expenditure bolstering family pride and thereby assuaging grief.

The same impetus exists in very poor communities, however. Showy Harlem funerals in the 1960s, were "often the only time when there is real luxury in the impoverished world of the racial ghetto," noted Michael Harrington in *The Other America*. "In 1950s Brazil, the first peasant league was formed, not to improve living conditions but to ensure for its members a coffin and a single grave", while poor Victorian families reserved one whole room of their miserable hovels for the formal lying in state of their dead. Even today, "traditional" funerals, particularly characteristic of the East End of London, follow the same pattern, with their horse-drawn hearses, flowers and top-hatted undertakers.

How different cultures talk through grief

The essence of bereavement, according to Dr Walter, writing in *Bereavement Care* (Spring 1991), is "for the community of people that knew the deceased to discuss and elaborate an accurate and durable biography, to develop a shared condensation of that person, mainly through conversation, so as to move on with, as well as without, the deceased".

The Jews understand this, he says. Jews bury the body within a day or so and then the close family "sit shiva". This involves them sitting in their living room at home for a week while friends, relatives and neighbours come to visit, bring food, talk about the departed, laugh, cry and share memories – until the week is over and the family slowly get back to ordinary life.

Talking is also an important part of bereavement in Muslim societies. The initial bereavement period lasts for three days, during which time prayers are recited almost continuously. From then on, however, there is continuing support from the extended family network. Shoes are taken off before entering the house of the bereaved, and it is customary to cover the head when talking about the person who has died, with relatives sitting on the carpet to pass on their condolences and tell stories about the deceased.

Oral expression of grief is also important in Greek Orthodox families, though it is done not through talking but through singing dirges, which lament the death. These dirges lead to an emotional outpouring that, according to the Greek Orthodox faith, "is meant to relieve the bereaved of the poisonous feelings of grief".

There is an increasing recognition that with mobile, urban societies, where fellow mourners live in different towns or countries, this talking tradition becomes more difficult, sometimes leading to a greater need for bereavement counselling. This recognition should also perhaps encourage people to make the extra effort that might be needed to talk to the bereaved more frequently.

How different cultures mark time

Marking the passing of time following the death is important in most cultures. The Jews recite Kaddish, an ancient hymn of praise to God, every day for a year following the funeral, and burn a candle at sundown exactly a year after the death. Greek Orthodox mourners say special prayers, or *mnemossina*, at three, nine and forty days and three, six, nine and twelve months after the death – and thereafter every year. The timing reflects the intensity of grief at the beginning of bereavement, and the gradual lessening of intensity in what is, nevertheless, a never-ending relationship with the dead person.

The end of mourning is also recognised in many traditional cultures. In rural Greece, there is a five-year period of mourning during which time the body lies in a temporary marble grave. At the end of that time, the bones are dug up and, provided they are clean, showing that the soul is now cleansed of sin and in paradise, they are buried in a communal village grave.

The Shona people of northern Zimbabwe take this physical manifestation of the process of bereavement further. Months of personal mourning are ended by the ceremony of "hitting the grave", to wake up the dead person's spirit in preparation for a final ceremony of "settling the spirit", inviting it to return to the community as one of the ancestors.

For Dr Walter, this ceremony makes good psychological and sociological sense. By affirming what is in reality already true, that the dead person lives on in the hearts of the community, the ceremony stresses the permanence of society and thereby, he says, "tames the intense personal pain of loss". However secular we become, he says, "we will never cease to believe that, in some way, the person does not die. We cannot but try to tame death". And that, perhaps, is the purpose of bereavement.

Gender and generational differences

While the culture we live in exerts a significant influence on the way we cope with bereavement, gender and generational differences are at least as great, possibly more so. At the extremes, men and women respond to loss in very different ways. And the post-war baby boomers, now coping with the death of aged parents, have a different response to grieving than an older generation.

The question of which form of bereavement is best, is not the point. Understanding how others feel, however, is inevitably a good development.

Gender differences

Cross-cultural studies suggest that that the biggest difference in the way people grieve is between men and women. Research from a major study of bereaved men and women in the Netherlands, has shown that –

- Women are more likely to have, and to appreciate, a social network that can offer them support. Men prefer to be seen as not needing such support and therefore do not build supportive networks.
- Women tend to express their emotions in every way: talking, singing (dirges) and crying. Men are, almost universally, more restrained than women – and in macho societies, restraint is an even more important code of behaviour.
- Women are more likely to become totally involved in their bereavement, albeit temporarily. Men tend to feel more comfortable throwing themselves into work or practical tasks from the very first days following the loss of a loved one.

There is a general view that women come off best in this division of emotional experience, based on the belief that crying is good for you and that being tight-lipped is old-fashioned and potentially dangerous. Recent research, however, suggests that this is not necessarily the case.

Men, it is true, tend to seek, and be offered far less emotional support from family, friends and professionals after the death of a loved one, and may suffer for it in the long-term. But while women are more likely to seek out, and receive, the counselling and the emotional support that is available, they may actually benefit more from receiving practical, problem-solving help during the period of grief.

Men … tend to seek, and be offered far less emotional support … and may suffer for it in the long-term … while women are more likely to seek out, and receive, the counselling and the emotional support that is available …

These findings emerged from the Netherlands study. It was originally set up to compare, on the one hand, the benefits of counselling to encourage the expression of emotion, with on the other hand, problem-solving cognitive behavioural therapy (CBT). The study found that there was no overall difference between the group of men and women who had counselling, and the group that had problem-solving CBT. But within each group, the researchers found major differences between men and women. Those men who were encouraged to express emotion did far better in the long-term than those who were encouraged to be practical – with the opposite being true of women.

"It makes sense if you think about it," explains Dr Murray-Parkes. "Women did not appear to benefit from being encouraged to express emotion. But they did manage better in the long-term when they were helped to develop problem-solving skills and address practical issues."

The value of this research is that it underlines that there is no single way of managing bereavement. At the same time, both men and women can benefit from being open to help from others.

Generational differences

Cruse, the bereavement charity, was set up in Britain to provide largely practical support for widows in the 1970s. Yet the largest group of people seeking help today are adult women and men whose elderly parent has died.

One might think that when grief is expected, it is less intense. Yet the death of a parent at any time is a turning point in the emotional, personal and social lives of most adults – and the potential for painful suffering should not be underestimated. Paradoxically, it may even be that the longer we have lived with our parents still alive, the harder it is when they eventually die. We have become so used to having them in our lives and to having an adult-to-adult relationship with them that their death can be shockingly painful.

Peter, 56, was devastated by the death of his mother at 85, after she had suffered from Parkinson's disease for 25 years: *"Why do people think it reasonable that she died at that point? Couldn't it have been two, five, ten years later? Several friends hoped I would be over it within a fortnight – not for my sake, for theirs. They were embarrassed at the thought of seeing me, a middle-aged man, going to pieces over the death of his mother. I went along with them and acted as though I was getting on with my life. I treated my fear, pain, loss and confusion as symptoms of a secret illness."*

Underpinning this embarrassment, perhaps, is simple ignorance. People no longer know how to behave when someone dies. "Children always assume that their loved ones will live forever," says John Morgan in his book *Death and Bereavement Around The World*. "But it's now possible to grow into adulthood without having to face the reality of death and dying. People don't really know what to do."

Attitudes to crying

Crying is an instinctive component of grief, starting from the very earliest hours of life. Yet it becomes a cultural option in adult life for a variety of reasons.

In war-like, "macho" communities, people of both sexes frequently repress any expression of emotion. In war-torn Rwanda, for instance, it is a badge of courage not to cry. Apaches in North America refuse to talk of the dead, making it a rule never to mention the name of a deceased parent.

Religious dogma may also forbid tears. Sikhs and some Christian fundamentalists forbid crying during bereavement as being anti-God. The fact that someone has died must be the will of God and to cry is to dispute with God.

There is also a view that crying is somehow a primitive, child-like response that is shameful in a civilised society. Both men and women in some British communities "get caught up in mourning as a test of control at a time when your cherished English reserve is most threatened," says Dr Walter.

And while crying may be acceptable in certain situations – for instance, the funeral and the cemetery – there remains a taboo on crying elsewhere in public or in front of a stranger. "Exerting self-control can come to be seen as an essential part of being civilised," says Dr Murray-Parkes. "The fear of being weak or not in control makes some people repress tears even in private."

Yet, he says, such attitudes are only skin deep and given the right role models, the most surprising people can and do weep openly, he says. "I once met an American gangster, very macho, very tight-lipped. He told me that when his mother died, he had been astonished to see his father crying at the funeral and that it was only then that the tears came and he was able to cry too. It's a question of permission."

The process of grieving

The grieving process, according to Dr Murray-Parkes, is about finding a way in which the dead person can live on in the memory of the bereaved person without imposing themselves on the reality of their lives. "It's about letting go of the 'outside' person and carrying forward the 'inside' person. It's a long process." Many people say that you never get over the death of loved one, you simply learn to live with it. You learn to realise that your relationship with the deceased will always be the same, that it can never be taken away from you, and that can be comforting.

Jan wrote long letters to her dead husband every day for two years, telling him what was happening to her and how she was coping. She finally stopped writing the letters to him on the night she married someone else. Writing the letters didn't stop her from moving on and actually meeting a new man in her life. But it kept her husband alive for her in a certain sense for as long as she needed – and at some point, that had to stop.

Accept help

People are frequently advised to keep going through the shock of grief. It is not necessarily a good idea. Just as with physical shock, rest and warmth are needed at a time when your emotional and physical health may be at a low ebb. Far from being a sign of not coping, accepting support from other people, including help with household chores, is a sign that you are taking seriously both your grief, and the death of a loved one.

Eventually you will no longer need that help and will find a new way of living (and working) that works for you. You will establish a routine that will prove very important in structuring your new life. The cliché that work (or any occupation that takes your mind off the situation) provides a raft to cling to is true for many people, though it is equally true that to throw oneself into work the minute a loved one has died only postpones a necessary grieving process.

Visit the grave

In the "lonely" weeks after the funeral and on the first anniversary, make arrangements to visit the grave with your co-bereaved, says Rabbi Julia Neuberger in her book, *Dying Well*. "It really helps to focus on the passage of time – and cemeteries are places where it is acceptable to weep," she says. Our increasingly fast-paced, secular society, with its lack of formal mourning rituals, finds it difficult to cope with people who do not quickly pull themselves together after a bereavement. The advantage of a cemetery is that there is no expectation for people to stay composed, nor to appear as if they have "got over" the death, however long before it might have occurred. On the contrary, it is a place where emotions can be given a totally free rein. Cemeteries can therefore provide much-needed relief from the everyday public mask that many people may be wearing for some time after the death of a loved one.

Go back to where the loved one died

It will almost certainly be an ordeal. But like so many ordeals, "it is eventually soothing, helping the process of letting go by what is known as reality testing," says bereavement specialist and author, Dr Colin Murray-Parkes. Many hospices and some hospitals hold services in their chapels once or twice a year for people whose relatives have died there during the preceding year. "We have been amazed that people travel long distances and bring their extended families and friends," says Suzi Croft, senior social worker at St John's Hospice in North London, which holds memorial teas twice a year.

Finding love after death

If you have lost your partner, you will know instinctively when you are ready to have another relationship with someone. You will find yourself engaging more with people, interacting with them emotionally, looking forwards, rather than backwards. There is no set timescale when it is OK to fall in love again. Everyone reacts differently and the speed at which they form a new relationship varies enormously.

There is some evidence, though, that the longer a grieving partner takes, the less likely they are to find someone to share their life with. As Dr Murray-Parkes says, "Grieving involves constant oscillation between missing the dead person intensely and what you had together in the past, and getting on with your life. As long as you do that, you'll come through the grieving process. It's the people caught at either extreme who get into difficulties."

There is some evidence ... that the longer a grieving partner takes, the less likely they are to find someone to share their life with.

When you do find yourself attracted to someone new, you should not worry that you will forget the dead person, or replace them. Nor are you betraying the love you had for that person. You will simply find another place in your heart for a new person, in the same way that parents always finds a place in their hearts to love every new child they have. It doesn't mean that they love their existing children a bit less; they love them all equally, though sometimes differently. It is the same with adult relationships following the death of a partner.

Helping children and teenagers to grieve for a parent

The loss of a parent for any child or teenager is devastating, however much warning they may have been given. It is difficult for them to comprehend how such a thing can happen, how unfair life suddenly now feels, and how unsafe. Why should this happen to them, to their mum, to their dad? Why can't they have a normal childhood, like everyone else? But there are ways to lessen the trauma. Much depends on who is around to help and support these children and teenagers, and how these various adults deal with the death. If the whole thing is worked through properly, the death can paradoxically enrich a young person's life. It will give them an understanding that life is precious and should never be taken for granted. They will gain a maturity beyond that of their peers and they may well be able to put the ups and downs of life into perspective, and be more philosophical about small mishaps. The death of a parent can often be the spur to make children and teenagers want to achieve something in their life, to "show" their dead parent what they are capable of.

The Whitbread prize-winning biographer, Amanda Foreman, says that she wishes her father, who died when she was 15, was able to witness what she has achieved: "*I want to say, 'Look, I did lots of degrees in history and I wrote a book'.*"

Ultimately, nothing can change the past. Even though death is always sad, it is part of life, and should be treated as such. All too often, when a young person loses a parent, it is the way that the death is handled (or mishandled) that harms them in the long term. But if the grieving process is handled well, it is vital to tell the bereaved child or teenager that the road they will take into adulthood need not be a worse one than if their parent was still alive – it will simply be a different one.

Children

Much of the advice given on pp. 62–7 regarding what to tell children whose loved one is dying (in particular when it is a parent) applies when helping them to grieve. Once again, the best advice is to be honest, and to be available to answer questions, however tactless, brutal or silly these might seem. It is important that children's routine is maintained as much as possible. The unshakeable security that life provided up until now has been shattered, so they need the safety net of their everyday routine if they are to feel safe in this unpredictable, frightening world. This does not mean pretending everything is the same as before, but it is vital that continuity is maintained in as many areas of a child's life as possible.

Children should attend the funeral of a loved one if at all possible. But if they are mourning the loss of a parent, this is vital, as this represents a transition for them, a way for them to understand the finality of the situation and a way for them to feel that their grief is as important as everyone else's. Ideally, and if those surrounding the child feel it is appropriate, children should also see the body of the deceased, firstly to establish some sort of closure, and secondly so that they can reassure themselves of the peaceful state that their loved one now finds themselves in. Clearly, a very young child may react very differently from a ten year-old, but children do have a vivid imagination and, if they are never allowed to view the body, they may become very worried and anxious as time progresses about what their loved one may have looked like in death.

Teenagers

Again, teenagers need openness and honesty from those surrounding them. They will feel betrayed if they subsequently discover that they were misinformed, and trust with that person will then be difficult to rebuild. Teenagers are at an age when they often start to communicate less and less with adults. If, in addition, they feel adults are not talking to them, or at least not telling them what they should be telling them, then they may not bother uttering anything more than the essential grunts required when they need feeding and clothing. And, as with children who often imagine the worst in a situation that has not been explained to them, teenagers will also tend to fill in the blanks and to blacken the picture more than may be necessary.

Bereaved teenagers still have the normal needs of teenagers – and the normal self-centredness – and it is important that that continuity is maintained. They should be allowed to go out, have fun, and argue with adults as much as any of their peers do. That, for them, represents their routine.

The teenager should view the body of the deceased person if at all possible, as this gives them a focus for their grieving. Also crucial is the funeral. Ideally, they should be involved, for example, by choosing the flowers or the music, or even by giving a reading. In this way, the funeral can bring closure to the situation. Also, teenagers can feel important in the process. All too often they get sidelined and are left to feel that what they want for this rite of passage is less important than what the grown-ups want and, by extension, that their grief is less important. And it is essential to understand that teenagers grieve by doing what they think people want them to do – by not being "difficult", for example – or by modelling their behaviour on that of their remaining parent, who is often desperate not to cry or break down in front of their children in order to protect them. Indeed, teenagers often appear to be doing incredibly well. Their school work does not suffer, and on the surface they behave as if nothing had happened. In short, they behave like adults. By not allowing them to talk, to take part in the funeral and in any subsequent grieving process, they end up bottling up their emotions and these simply come out in years to come.

Dos and don'ts of helping a bereaved child and teenager

- Do give them clear information about the death. What they are not told, they will imagine.

- Do keep them involved – this is especially important for the funeral.

- Do continue their routine – allow them to play, to laugh, to have tantrums.

- Do listen to their fears and their fantasies, and answer their questions honestly.

- Do let them say what they are feeling, however inappropriate these emotions may seem.

- Don't protect them from their pain with a conspiracy of silence.

- Do show teenagers that it is all right to cry by crying yourself and showing your emotions.

- Do reassure young children that they were not the cause of the death.

- Do explain to them that their life will not be worse, it will simply be different.

The importance of talking

Knowing what to say when someone has died is not easy: there seems to be a risk of getting it wrong and of possibly causing more hurt and upset. For many people, it is easier to avoid mentioning the name of the person who has died, out of fear that it will bring back upsetting memories for those who are mourning. Yet, while everyone grieves in his or her own individual way, almost all the bereaved want to talk about the loved one that is now deceased. Bereaved people, it is now understood, are not trying to break their life-long bond with the dead person in the process of going through their grief: that person will never – and should never – disappear from their memories. A "successful" bereavement involves people finding a place for the dead person in their memory, as part of their ongoing life. A widow will remember the joy of her marriage, as well as the grief following the death, while getting on with her life. A bereaved parent will talk of having three children, one of whom has died.

The sports journalist, Matthew Engel, writing about the most bitter loss, the death of his teenage son from cancer, acknowledged that neither he nor his wife, Hilary, would ever "get over it":

"We don't want to get over it. The challenge is to ensure that we can accept Laurie's death into the narrative of our lives without destroying everything else that we touch."

Talking about the deceased with other people – whether they are friends or relatives, a counsellor or a new acquaintance – is an essential part of the process. If those other people avoid the subject, it can seem to the bereaved person that they have forgotten their loss. Instead of feeling buoyed up by the support of others, they are more likely to feel isolated, frightened and confused, alongside the painful feelings of grief.

Talking about the deceased with other people … is an essential part of the process.

Julia, 47, joined the support group, Compassionate Friends, when she was unable to talk about her bereavement to friends or family, who believed such conversations were not helping her get over the death of her daughter.

"My sister is the worst. She hangs up on me when I mention her name."

That is not to say the bereaved will welcome any opportunity to discuss the deceased. They may very well seem prickly and uninviting, particularly if the opening gambit seems clichéd or patronising. When someone is bereaved, sensitivity and consideration from friends, colleagues and neighbours is of great value.

Try hard not to say any of the phrases below:

- buck up
- think of the kids
- pull yourself together
- every cloud's got a silver lining
- it's God's will
- it's fate
- it only takes time
- you're young enough – you can get married again and have another baby
- anyway, she had a good innings.

All of these imply that the bereaved has to sever their relationship with the deceased and get on with life. That is neither helpful nor realistic.

"I know what you're going through" or *"I know how you feel"* more or less invite the response *"You almost certainly do not."* For the bereaved, especially when the deceased is a spouse, child or parent, the experience is often unexpectedly intense and unprecedented. Anything that compares the person's loss with someone else's implies that the mourning is somehow routine, and this can be hurtful.

Everybody has their own way of coping and it can sometimes help people to be "in denial", and not to feel grief until they are ready to handle it. Yet, it is commonplace for a bereaved person to be told, *"You should have got over it by now"* or *"It will help you to cry. I am concerned that you have not shed tears for her."* Anything that judges the way people are grieving is also unhelpful.

How should you discuss the deceased?

The simplest rule is to follow the lead of the grieving person and that will often mean him or her doing the talking, and you doing the listening.

> *"I wanted to say 'Don't tell me what I should be feeling or what you expect me to be feeling. Ask me how I am feeling and let me tell you. And then I will feel that you care'."* **June, 33,** commenting on the way people passed on their expectations of how she was feeling in the weeks after her mother's death.

It may be difficult to be with someone who is bereaved without giving them advice or trying to cheer them up. But the way to help at this time will often be to let the person express their feelings and thoughts about the deceased person, often with stories about their life together, some sad, some joyful. If you don't know what to say, or don't even know whether to talk about it or not, be honest and say so. "I'm sorry, I don't know what to say" may sound pointless, but it is a first step and encourages the grieving person to talk to you and to tell you whatever he or she wants. Just be a listening ear, the friend who is not uncomfortable talking about grief and loss. And if the bereaved person does cry, don't be embarrassed; tell yourself rather that they are doing so because they feel comfortable enough in your presence to show their emotions. It is a sign that they value your friendship and your support.

Be aware that the bereaved may still feel in contact with the deceased. Though there is little research into the subject, talking to the dead is probably far more common than is acknowledged, both in the early weeks of intense grief, and later on as life goes on.

It is very common for the bereaved to "see" the dead person in the street or in the park, for months after the death. Visiting a spiritualist medium can seem to be a reasonable way of getting in touch with the dead for bereaved people who would normally laugh at such an idea. Older widows frequently talk to their husbands as though they were still alive, while men are known to go the cemetery "to have a chat with the lad" or to tell a spouse about the birth of a new grandchild.

When Julie's father died after a long illness, she was worried that her mother seemed to think that her husband was still in the house, watching TV with her or helping her make tea: *"She didn't get upset when he died as my sisters and I did. She seemed to accept it quite calmly which I found very hard to bear. It was only when I talked to a bereavement counsellor that I found out that this is quite common: it is an initial denial or reluctance to accept that the death has actually happened. It seems that this is actually a defence mechanism and that my mother was trying to avoid facing the reality of the loss at a time when she couldn't cope with it. Understanding that made it easier for us all to continue talking about my dad."*

Don't be surprised if you have heard it all before. There is considerable evidence that one way of coping with loss is to go over the same ground again and again. It can be the mark of a true friend or loving relative to be able to sit and listen without interruption to whatever that person wants to say — for as long as he or she wants to go on saying it. Bereavement counsellors recognise that it is only by talking that a bereaved person can see all the different angles and aspects of what has happened and, perhaps, gradually learn to deal with the painful images of the death and focus on the happy memories of their lives together.

Keeping the door open

After someone's death, the bereaved sometimes find themselves becoming increasingly isolated. This may not happen at once. And in the days following the death, during which time they are probably organising the funeral and informing others of the death, they may be too busy to notice. They are surrounded by well-meaning people who are doing their best to offer comfort and support at a most difficult time.

It is after the funeral and burial that visitors often stop calling and the phone stops ringing. Yet, all too often, this is the time when the bereaved suddenly feel the aching void and a growing sense of loneliness. At night, the family home may feel strange and empty, whereas during the day, it may feel too quiet, giving rise to an overwhelming sense of loss.

It is after the funeral and burial that visitors often stop calling and the phone stops ringing.

In addition, if the bereaved was nursing a loved one through a long illness, the sense of loss can be even greater. There would have been days when, tired and drained by the constant demands of the patient, they felt that life was one long round of washing, feeding, dressing and washing, and they secretly wished it could all be over quickly (with all the guilt that those feelings would have given them). Even so, the very fact that the bereaved had been so involved with the care of the dying person and had no time for themselves, now presents them with a shocking new set of circumstances: life suddenly feels very empty.

Despite this, it may be very hard for the bereaved to return to the life they once had, before their loved one fell ill. They are unable to restart the hobbies and activities that they once pursued, or to meet up with friends they used to like seeing. The bereaved need a lot of help and support in the days and weeks following the death of a loved one. Don't rush them, but try gently and patiently to get them to go out a little and to begin to show a bit of interest once more in pastimes and activities that they used to enjoy. Make sure also that you pick up the phone and keep in touch with them. In this way, you will help the bereaved person to face the world again.

Special days and anniversaries

These occasions can be particularly painful: most of all because they are a reminder of the deceased person's absence, and the fact that "this is it", that the deceased person is not coming back. Life has taken you along a different path from the one you were expecting and special days can be moments when you cannot help but glance across at what the other road might have been. It is not just festive occasions that can be difficult, but also wedding anniversaries, birthdays, and above all the anniversary of the death itself. Sometimes, unexpected minor events – even seeing an old photograph – can be enough to open the lid and release the grief from inside the box where it is normally kept. These are all times when memories are likely to be particularly resonant and ruminations painful: what kind of a grandparent might that parent have become if they had still been alive? How might a couple have been celebrating the anniversary if one spouse had not died?

"It can be so difficult to stay cheerful at Christmas for the children. You wrap the presents and remember the daft jokes he'd make or the help you'd get with the shopping that now you have to do alone. The door bell went the other day and it was the brass band playing carols. I sobbed and sobbed. I couldn't stop. Somehow the music was a trigger for something that went very deep indeed." Helen, 57.

Bereaved people clearly need extra support and thoughtfulness at these times. It doesn't always happen: the journalist Lindsay Nicholson, who lost her husband and later one of her children, wrote an article in the *Mail on Sunday* saying that she now visits their graves a day or two before the anniversaries, ever since a former colleague remarked that she was surprised not to have seen any fresh flowers when she had visited.

"I had brought flowers, of course, but arrived later than her. As chief mourner, you are appointed keeper of the flame and other people feel badly if you don't behave in a way they think is fitting, however rough you may be feeling."

What's more, anticipating that an anniversary is going to be difficult doesn't always protect you from the shock and horror of it. For many people, the picture of bereavement is summed up by the vague wistfulness of the *In Memoriam* notices that appear in newspapers on the anniversary of someone's death, of the "Though absent, you are always near/Still loved and missed and very dear" variety. The reality can be very different.

"You expect that the anniversary is going to be bad, and so you try to protect yourself. I spent the second anniversary of Roger's death with his mother and threw red roses in the sea. I felt quite peaceful that day, as though perhaps I had reached some kind of closure. It was the next day that the 'foreverness' suddenly hit me. Our relationship wasn't always easy but we'd been together for 35 years and his dying has caused me such pain in so many unexpected ways. It just felt as though this was going to be the rest of my life and that seemed unbearable." Helen, 57.

Yet it is this very intensity that can signal the beginning of a new, more comfortable life, a recognition that, although life will never be the same again, that there is a bright and welcoming future.

Talking about the present and future

The first year of bereavement is more than simply a period of grief following the death of the loved one. It is also a state of being caught between the present, the past and a lost future, between an old, familiar situation and a new, unfamiliar and probably unwanted situation. Time heals all and the intense pain is almost certainly temporary.

In the first year of bereavement, however, that does not mean very much. As the saying goes, "In life, when one door closes, another always opens … but the hallways are a bitch." Getting through this painful time is likely to involve recalling the past relationship with the person who has died in order to create a much-needed new relationship: this time with the deceased. The world has to be "re-learnt": as a child (even a middle-aged child) without a parent, a spouse without a partner, a parent who has lost a child. An important part of this process involves facing up to the difference between the future that was planned or might have happened if the deceased were still alive, and the unknown future.

It is hardly surprising that facing up to these new truths, frequently involving new financial difficulties, loneliness, sheer exhaustion and fear of the future, involves a roller-coaster of emotions. What begins with numbness and denial, progresses and frequently develops over the first month into a state of agitation, anger, anxiety and irritation. There can be long periods of depression along with guilt that somehow the death could have been prevented. All of these emotions are frequently deep and intense and affect people in different ways and at different times, ebbing and flowing without any apparent logical sequence. What is more, the new present can change the picture of the deceased, sometimes in small ways, sometimes more significantly. The weeks after the death can be a time of learning: from photographs, diaries, even letters of condolence from colleagues at work, friends from the past or distant relations.

… emotions are frequently deep and intense and affect people in different ways and at different times, ebbing and flowing without any apparent logical sequence.

Bereavement counselling, which has become far more widely available over the last few years, is probably so much in demand because it gives people the space and time to talk in detail about the deceased person, and about the future that might have been. Whereas in the past, people talked to their parish priest or to their extended family, nowadays many people live a more isolated life, which is perhaps why there is a much greater need for "neutral" counsellors who can listen to them when they are going through a difficult time.

Cruse, the bereavement charity, was contacted by 170,000 people in 2004. As well as providing one-to-one support and advice, it organises group support meetings throughout the UK. These, says the charity, are increasingly seen as the best means of support, enabling people to share their experiences with people who have suffered similar losses.

Bereavement counsellors see their job as listening to the bereaved person talking about their pain and grief about the deceased person and gradually, perhaps, moving on to other matters. Over a period of time, perhaps a year, perhaps longer, the bereaved person will begin to show signs of moving into the "real" future, recognising that there is no going back, perhaps throwing out the clothes, making plans, enrolling on a course, booking a holiday. As one counsellor explained, "It's not a matter of telling someone 'The sooner you go out to dinner, the sooner you'll get over your grief'. It's more about allowing the person to return to a social life at their own pace – and helping them keep track of their progress." Gradually, the lid from the box that contains the grief opens less often, and less violently. The bereaved learn to look around them, to take pleasure once more in the world around them, and in those people – friends and family – who have supported them all along.

Chapter 5 Funerals and memorial services

If you think of a funeral simply as an occasion to bury a dead person, think again. It is a complicated event that means different things to different people. It is a time when the deceased person's life is remembered with joy and respect, as well as an opportunity for the bereaved to join together in an expression of their grief; it is a recognition that one life has ended and that, for the bereaved, another is beginning; it can be an extravagant display of status and wealth or managed on a shoestring. For some, the aim of the funeral is to comfort the bereaved. For others, it is an opportunity to say prayers for the soul of the departed. There are interfaith ceremonies, humanist ceremonies and a growing interest in fully or partly do-it-yourself funerals that are built on an awareness of individual spirituality and a desire to get involved.

From death to funeral

A funeral should be viewed as a final testimony to a person, a way for family and friends to make a statement that something significant has happened: that a human life has ended. In his book, *Funerals And How To Improve Them* (Hodder & Stoughton), sociologist Dr Tony Walter makes the point that a funeral needs to "say the unsayable, marking the passing of a human life with sorrow but also with integrity, mourning the death while also giving hope for the future". Good funerals mingle sorrow with joy, perplexity with faith, unique pain with support from friends. They create sharing where there had been isolation, allow anger to be expressed while also enabling mutual forgiveness.

Funerals are sometimes described as a time of closure after the shock of the death of a loved one. Yet a funeral within days of the death, may be far too early for any feeling of completion. The death of someone in a close family changes the relationships between the remaining members, creating an emotional limbo. Arranging and attending the funeral both give the bereaved something to do while in this limbo, providing a transition time, a time to adjust. It is a rite of passage where people can come together publicly to express respect and love, to say goodbye and be supported.

Embalming and cleaning of the body

Undertakers, or funeral directors, usually prepare the body (unless the deceased is of a religion where there are particular rites associated with death and with the preparation of bodies). Whether or not relatives or friends will be viewing the body, the undertakers' procedures will be exactly the same. Most funeral directors embalm, unless asked not to.

There are a number of reasons for embalming. Firstly, in order to preserve the body until it is either buried or cremated, in other words, until the time of committal. Secondly, embalming protects the public and the funeral director's staff from any health risks that might otherwise occur. Finally, and perhaps most importantly, embalming is the most effective way of presenting the deceased in a dignified and peaceful state – one that often provides the most lasting image for loved ones. This is the image that will contrast with the one you may have seen immediately prior to, or following, death.

The embalming process consists of making small incisions into a suitable artery and injecting a specially prepared fluid based on formaldehyde into the vascular system, thus draining a small amount of blood in return. This fluid enters the arteries and penetrates the tissues, which temporarily arrests decomposition. The time involved in this procedure varies, depending on cause of death, age and condition of the deceased. If the deceased has been subjected to a post-mortem examination, the procedure will be different and can take longer to perform.

In rare instances, embalming can be carried out at the deceased's home. However, this is not desirable, because any problems that might arise are best dealt with in the preparation room or mortuary, where all proper facilities are readily available.

Embalming is carried out only after two doctors have completed forms B and C (in the case of cremation) or when the funeral director has in his possession **a.** *the registration certificate,* or **b.** *the coroner's Order for Burial/Certificate E* for cremation.

... embalming is the most effective way of presenting the deceased in a dignified and peaceful state

Preparing to see a body

One of the mysteries surrounding death, and one which can cause worry and anxiety among the next-of-kin, concerns what happens to the deceased's body once they have died. Despite what many people think, for example, it is unusual for bodily fluids to be secreted from the body after death. Equally, when it comes to the appearance of a dead body, this too is shrouded in secrecy, possibly because we are now so unused to death in our society that we rarely talk about such matters. Inevitably, many people are very concerned about what they will find if and when they do see a dead body.

Rigor mortis is a temporary situation that causes much anxiety and even fear amongst the bereaved when they are faced with the prospect of viewing the body of their loved one. In reality, rigor mortis sets in 6–18 hours after death and will disappear within 24 hours, never to return. It is one of life's mysteries and, even today, doctors have failed to give an unequivocal medical reason for why it happens. Outwardly, however, a body that is in the rigor mortis stage looks identical to one that is not. It simply feels hard to the touch and, like all dead bodies, cold.

Following hygienic treatment, the deceased will be dressed either in a nightgown/dressing gown or, as is often the case nowadays, in his or her own clothes. Funeral directors or those who prepare the body must take particular care with the physical appearance of the deceased, irrespective of whether family and friends wish to view the body and pay their last respects, because this inevitably becomes a focal point for their grief. As a result –

- hair is always neatly combed
- fingernails are always clean
- men must be clean-shaven (hair and nails continue to grow in the hours immediately after death, so men would appear unshaven if not attended to properly)
- make-up is only applied if specifically requested by next-of-kin, otherwise, those preparing the body will simply ensure that the face looks as natural as possible.

Release of the body

There are various procedures that need to be arranged in order to secure the release of the deceased from the place where they died to the funeral home. There is no doubt that, for grieving relatives, one of the primary considerations is for this procedure to be carried out as quickly as possible. Sadly, though, this is not the only consideration.

There are practical issues to be addressed: for example, how tall/wide is the deceased. Coffins do not come in standard sizes, any more than human beings do, and, although the funeral director will have many in stock, he will need to establish which size is needed. Most hospital mortuary staff are very good about passing this information on to the funeral director prior to release of the body, and this enables preparations to be undertaken as quickly as possible.

There are other criteria to be met before release of the body. Has the death been registered? If so, has the person registering the death handed the green "disposal" certificate to the funeral director (or person organising the funeral) authorising the removal and preparation of the body? On occasion, there is an additional requirement: a hospital may issue a Hospital Removal form, to be signed by next-of-kin and, while the form alone will not suffice, it must be produced together with the green form, by the funeral director's staff, prior to release of the body.

Currently the term "Disposal Certificate" appears on the green form, suggesting an act of throwing away/getting rid of something – not at all what funerals are about. The simple words "Funeral Certificate" would be more appropriate.

If the funeral arrangements are to include cremation, it is necessary for two doctors to complete medical certificates B and C. These are statutory forms and require the body to be visually examined by both doctors. The forms are usually arranged by the hospital bereavement services and then collected by the funeral director who will send or deliver them to the crematorium. Because each doctor examines the body independently of the other and the second only does so after he has spoken with his counterpart, it is not unusual to wait up to 48 hours for the forms to be completed.

When a death has been reported to the coroner's office, it is not possible to remove the deceased from the hospital until the coroner gives authority, making available at the same time a Burial Order, or a Certificate E for cremation.

Reasons for an autopsy and/or an inquest

A coroner can order a post-mortem examination. He/she needs neither permission nor agreement from next-of-kin to do so. However, if a medical practitioner makes a similar request, he/she *must* obtain permission from close relatives.

A coroner can order a post-mortem examination. He or she needs neither permission nor agreement from next-of-kin to do so.

"'Autopsy" and "post-mortem" are terms that can be used interchangeably. The discovery that a coroner has ordered a post-mortem examination and, subsequently, an inquest into a death understandably causes alarm to the deceased person's next-of-kin but it is always as a result of a specific set of circumstances.

Based on the information gathered, the Coroner will decide whether or not an inquest should follow. If the post-mortem examination finds cause of death to be natural – heart attack, cancer, effects of chronic disease or even, as sometimes happens, as a result of a hitherto undetected medical condition – an inquest will not be necessary.

Where research is being carried out in a particular field and the medical practitioner believes examination of the deceased patient's condition will be of use to scientists and researchers, he/she might request a post-mortem examination but only after

a. he/she has issued a "cause of death" medical certificate and **b.** obtained written consent from next-of-kin.

Usually, the Registrar or attending doctor reports the (unnatural) death to the Coroner's Office. But anyone – family, friend, neighbour, police – who has knowledge of the deceased person and believes his/her death to be unnatural, has a duty to report it to the Coroner.

Where death occurs at home, it is usual for the medical practitioner who has cared for the deceased during his or her last illness to sign the death certificate and it will normally be available for the family to collect from the surgery within a few hours. Thereafter, removal of the body to the funeral home can take place quickly.

In general a death is reported to the Coroner's Office if –

- it is unexpected
- it arises out of an act of violence
- it is thought to be as a result of privation or neglect
- it occurs in suspicious circumstances.

However, if the deceased person has not been attended by a medical practitioner in the 14 days prior to death, the death is reported to the Coroner's Office. The funeral director would then be instructed to remove the body to the local mortuary appointed by the coroner's office. He/she will then make enquiries with the deceased's doctor and if, as a result of those enquiries, he is satisfied the death is neither unnatural nor suspicious, he can authorise the issue of the death certificate.

When the time comes to remove the body from a hospital to the funeral home, undertakers are sometimes presented with a difficulty: larger hospitals often restrict the hours in which they can attend the mortuary and, if these times coincide with the hours when they would normally expect to be arranging or conducting funerals, such restrictions can and do present the funeral directors with logistical problems regarding vehicles and staff.

The mortuary

"Mortuary" is rather a stark name for a storage facility where bodies are kept in a secure temperature-controlled environment until all legal requirements are completed, after which the body can be released to the funeral director or to whoever is organising the funeral.

Most hospitals have purpose-built facilities, with fully trained staff, whose duties include receiving bodies, preparing them for identification purposes, post-mortem duties where necessary, and ultimate release of the deceased to the appointed funeral director. Mortuary staff are also responsible for detailing personal effects such as jewellery and cash, which may have arrived with the deceased.

In smaller, cottage hospitals it is usual for the deceased to be kept in a refrigerated cabinet, in a small, unmanned room. In such cases, the hospital porter releases the body as part of his/her duties.

Some larger hospices have similar purpose-built mortuary facilities, though most hospices today are more involved in providing respite care for people with long-term illness than providing end-of-life care. Nursing homes are unlikely to have a mortuary. In these cases, once a doctor has declared life extinct, a call is made to the funeral director nominated by immediate family or whose details may already be held on file by the nursing home, in accordance with the deceased person's known wishes. The funeral director will then remove the body to the funeral home.

Some funeral homes prefer to use the term "preparation room", rather than the word "mortuary", as it better conveys what happens there. The preparation room is usually divided into two distinct areas: one part houses the temperature-controlled facility, where the first duty of the undertakers is to attach their own wristlet to the body for identification purposes; the second area is reserved for preparation, including hygienic treatment, or embalming.

Most hospital mortuaries have been upgraded and include disinfectant foot trays, automatic soap dispensers and water taps, all designed to prevent potential infections or hazards spreading beyond the mortuary. Funeral home mortuaries are similarly careful about hygiene and have strict procedures to ensure that there are no health risks to anyone who comes into contact with the deceased.

Where death occurs in hospital, relatives are, if they so wish, able to view the body of their loved one when they are in the hospital mortuary. Indeed, bigger hospitals would usually have a small chapel or side room to where the body can be brought. It

Procedures for release of body to funeral home

- Death must be registered (*see p. 153*) or Coroner's certificate E for cremation or Burial Order must be obtained.

- Person registering the death to hand green "Disposal Certificate" (obtained upon registering of death) to funeral director, or to person organising funeral. This authorises removal of body to funeral home.

- If body is to be cremated, two doctors to complete medical certificates B and C. These certificates to be collected by funeral director.

- If death occurs at home, body would be removed to funeral home as soon as death certificate signed by medical practitioner. If cremation was then required, the two doctors needed to complete certificates B and C would examine the body at the funeral home.

- No funeral arrangements can be made until death has been registered.

will not be in a coffin but will more likely be lying on a tray and covered with a white sheet. The Hospital Bereavement Services are responsible for the preparation of all necessary documentation, and they act as speedily as possible in order to complete the formalities that allow the transfer of the body to the appointed funeral home. These services play a vital role in the funeral director's preparations.

Dealing with Death Certificates and administrative requirements

Registration of death is the only function that cannot be performed by the funeral director. It is a legal requirement that an immediate family member must undertake that particular duty or, in the absence of any close relatives, the executor or solicitor may do so.

Until registration has been completed, no firm funeral arrangements can be made. Everything is dependent upon death registration, other than when the Coroner is involved, in which case he/she will determine if and when registration can take place.

Registration usually takes place in the area where death occurs but, in exceptional circumstances it can be completed by declaration. This means that registration is done in another area from the one where the death occurred, after which the relevant forms and certificates are posted to the correct area. This would only apply, for example, when the next-of-kin is old and/or infirm and unable to travel, or lives too far away to address the matter in person. To register by declaration does inevitably delay the funeral.

Under Section 16(3) of the Births & Deaths Registration Act 1953, a death must be registered within five days of having occurred, except where certain circumstances allow the period to be extended to 14 days: for example, if the next-of-kin are abroad and unable to return within the required time.

Nowadays, many register offices have an appointment system in place but, in all cases, the registrar will need to have sight of the following documentation –

1   medical certificate (Death Certificate) issued by the GP, who will have attended during the deceased's last illness
2   full name and surname of deceased and, in the case of a married woman, her maiden name
3   date and place of birth if female (or male if name is not that registered at birth) and, in the case of a deceased widow, full name and occupation of her late husband
4   if married (male or female), date of birth of surviving spouse
5   full address at which the deceased usually resided
6   evidence that the deceased was in receipt of state pension/benefits
7   full name and surname of the informant (person registering death); qualification – i.e. relative, executor; usual address.

Once documentation is authenticated, the person registering will sign the register, thus certifying to the registrar that the information given is correct.

The registrar can then issue the following –

1   registrar's certificate for burial or cremation (Disposal Certificate)
2   Certificate of Registration of Death – for benefits agency purposes
3   copies of the entry in the register (for private purposes such as solicitor, bank, insurer) and for which payment for each copy is necessary.

Who is eligible to register a death?

Those eligible to register deaths that have occurred in the home, nursing homes or other sorts of care homes are –

- a relative of the deceased present at death
- a relative in attendance during the deceased's last illness
- a relative living or being in the sub-district where death occurred
- a person present at death
- any inmate, if he/she knew of the happening of the death
- the occupier, if he/she knew of the happening of the death*
- the person causing disposal of the body, i.e. charged with making the arrangements. For example, the person or executor responsible for payment of the account

*The occupier in this instance relates to public institutions, and includes a governor, keeper, master, matron, superintendent or other chief resident officer.

Those eligible to register deaths not in houses, or dead bodies found, include –

- any relative of the deceased who knows any of the particulars required to register
- any person present at death
- any person who found the body
- any person in charge of the body
- person causing disposal of the body

In certain cases, the Registrar may refuse to register death without first consulting the Coroner, and in such cases, it is advisable to inform your funeral director, who may be able to offer advice.

It is often the case that the deceased person who has lived and worked away from his or her birth place will at some time have expressed a desire that his or her body be returned to his or her place of origin for burial or cremation. The family may also wish this to be the case. Either way, this can be easily arranged with the help of a funeral director who is either a member of the National Association of Funeral Directors, the Society of Allied & Independent Funeral Directors or the British Institute of Funeral Directors, all of which are recognised organisations striving to maintain and improve the care of the deceased and support for the bereaved.

If the deceased is to be repatriated to Scotland or abroad, a Coroner's "Out of England" certificate is needed, together with a certificate of embalming. For bodies being repatriated abroad, special coffins with zinc linings have to be arranged and these are only sealed in the presence of a customs officer who comes to the funeral parlour in person to witness the sealing.

Death that occurs in another country must be reported to the Coroner's Office, either at the point of entry into the UK (an airport, or a port) or at the final resting place of the deceased. Similarly, although documentation accompanying the deceased may be in a language other than English, and may have no translation, it too must be delivered to that same Coroner's Office. Once the Coroner has given clearance, the funeral can proceed without delay. Often, UK-based international funeral directors will make all the necessary arrangements to repatriate the body, something that can be done fairly swiftly, particularly if the death occurred in another EU country. Once the body is back in the UK, local funeral directors then take over all further arrangements.

The death itself will not be registered in the UK but rather in the country in which it took place. Subsequently, relatives wanting copies of the Death Certificate will have to apply to the British Consulate in that country.

What are the options?

Organising a funeral can often appear to come down to a handful of choices: cremation or burial; C of E or Catholic. Yet it does not have to be like that. There are almost no restrictions on funerals today. The only regulations around a death are that –

- it has to be certified by a doctor or Coroner
- it has to be registered with a Registrar of Births, Marriages and Deaths
- the body should either be cremated or buried.

There is no legal requirement –

- to have a funeral at all

- to hold a funeral in a licensed building: unless you want an Anglican service in England, for example, both religious or non-religious funeral services can be held at home
- to use a clergyman
- to use an undertaker
- to use a coffin: the body can simply be wrapped in a shroud.

Few people are likely to wish to take over the entire management of the funeral of a loved person at a time when they have just been bereaved. Yet it can be desirable, even therapeutic, to take charge of one or more aspects of the funeral management. Good funeral directors are aware that there is an increasing desire to participate in organising the funeral of a loved person, and many now see themselves as facilitators to help relatives and friends create a ceremony that they will look back on with positive, rather than negative feelings.

What the funeral director offers

Good funeral directors do not adopt the "one size fits all" approach that is prevalent in many service industries today. A "good" funeral must reflect the wishes of the family and be in keeping with the wishes of the deceased if they have been documented – or what relatives feel would have been the deceased's wishes, if they have not been made explicit.

Sometimes, the family will come to the funeral home to make the arrangements but, ideally, it is best if the funeral director can call on them at home. A good funeral director will take care to put people at their ease and to help them feel in control of events. He will also be aware that there may be a certain amount of resentment against a professional making a living out of other people's misery. This feeling is understandable (if quite unreasonable) but is almost always dispelled as the funeral director creates a relationship between himself and the bereaved.

Having taken note as relatives talked about the loved one's illness and subsequent death, and listened as they recalled fond memories, the funeral director will begin asking for the necessary details: did the deceased leave any instructions regarding his or her funeral and, if not, have the next-of-kin had the opportunity to discuss matters among themselves?

It is important that the bereaved do not feel rushed at this stage. Often, the funeral director will simply deal with the preliminaries at that first meeting: full name, age and address of the deceased, occupation (current or prior to retirement), date and time of death, name of the family practitioner, the deceased's religion (if relevant), are you considering burial or cremation, will you want a religious service. These areas can be dealt with at that initial meeting, and this allows the funeral director to return to his office and begin his own preparations.

At this stage, the funeral director may leave you to think about the more detailed elements of the funeral and burial, including –

- wording for obituary notices
- hymns or music to be sung
- flowers – he may leave a brochure that contains not simply depictions of the various floral tributes, but a selection of verses or wording suitable for the obituary or flower card
- number of limousines required (or horse-drawn carriages, if desired)
- in the case of cremation, what is to be done with the remains: will they be scattered, interred in the local cemetery or churchyard for example, or might they be taken out of the country at a future date?

These things are not usually uppermost in the minds of grieving relatives. They are usually more concerned with how soon they can bring the deceased from the hospital to the funeral home; what day the funeral is likely to be; and when can they come to the chapel of rest to say their farewells. Consequently, a barrage of questions at this stage on the part of the funeral director is not generally very helpful.

Of course, there are exceptions to the rule: sometimes next-of-kin will want to move things along quite quickly, particularly if they have travelled some distance to register the death and meet the funeral director. If they have young families or work commitments, they will hope that the funeral director can get as much done on their behalf as possible on the day, so that they may travel home, safe in the knowledge that everything is being taken care of as it should. The funeral director will then make a point of keeping in contact with the person(s) from whom they have taken instruction, via the phone or email.

Traditional funerals and burials

If the wishes of the family are for a traditional burial, the funeral director will have established whether there is an existing family grave that must be re-opened by cemetery/ churchyard staff or if he is to give instruction for a new grave to be dug and, if so, one depth or two? Is there a memorial at the grave site, in which case, will it have to be removed to facilitate burial?

Back at the office, the funeral director can contact the appropriate authority and book a day and time for the funeral. Then he will arrange for a minister of the deceased's religion to be available on that day, if that is what is required. Occasionally, the availability of the minister will not coincide with the cemetery opening hours, some of which can be quite restricted, and the funeral director has to look again at times and dates agreeable to both minister and local authority.

If the deceased's family has opted for cremation, the statutory requirements discussed above, in the "Release of the body" section, must be fulfilled.

When the family is ready to continue with arrangements, there are a number of issues to address. With regard to press notices, particular care is taken with spellings. Failure to do so implies a lack of concern on the part of the funeral director and, surprisingly, some families have never properly considered the spellings of names, particularly those of grandchildren and great-grandchildren, so they are grateful when time and trouble is taken to help in these apparently minor details.

When it comes to the formalities surrounding the funeral, it is important to point out that, having taken careful note of the requirements, the funeral director should make arrangements without fuss and without referring back unnecessarily to the family. They have undertaken the one task that the funeral director cannot perform on their behalf – that of registering the death. Now he must do his part to ensure that the last act of the bereaved is to pay fitting tribute to a loved one with a service that embraces care, compassion, dignity, a lot of warmth and even (when required) humour. The family should be left with, if not a happy memory, at least a sense that things were done properly and well.

When the various tasks have been completed – such as booking the date and time with the crematorium or cemetery staff, arranging the minister, if relevant, making certain the correct forms are ordered – the funeral director can telephone next-of-kin and confirm all details. This is followed up with a typewritten funeral arrangement card that sets out clearly, for example, the number of limousines in the cortege, times for departure from the house (or the time when family and friends should assemble if the cortege is

Traditional coffins and caskets

These vary greatly in shape, colour and materials. Certain
restrictions apply if cremation is to take place, though not if burial
has been decided upon.

Traditionally, the coffin used for cremation will be made from particle board
and covered with a thin layer of veneer made of natural timber such as oak
or elm. The particle board is made from wood chips, and is usually the residue
of machined timber.

For the purpose of cremation, the coffin is made of materials that are then
subjected to intense heat, so they must not give off smoke or toxic gas. Metal
furniture (such as handles, crucifix and name plate) is not allowed, nor is the
use of metal screws in the construction. Products containing PVC, either
inside or outside the coffin are also ruled out. The only exception is the name
plate which can be made from polystyrene. Similar restrictions apply to coffin
linings: sawdust, cotton wool, lead and zinc cannot be used, and specialist
manufacturers supply lining materials that are not harmful to the environment.

All these coffins can also be used for burial. However, you may prefer to
opt for a more traditional solid oak, elm, cherry wood or other timber coffin or
casket. Often, these coffins will be very ornate, with carvings, solid brass or
bronze handles and lavish silken interiors. You can rest assured, however, that
the funeral director will not put any pressure on you to choose an expensive
option. Nor should you feel under moral obligation to splash out on an
extravagant coffin.

Ultimately, it all comes down to personal choice. Every option is available
and, ideally, the next-of-kin will have some idea of how much they want to
spend and what sort of coffin or casket they would like (*see also p.167 for
more unusual and personalised styles of coffin*).

leaving from the funeral home, or when mourners should meet at the place of worship or
crematorium) and all other details for the service and/or burial. It may seem only a small
thing and perhaps an unnecessary one, given that the family has already been verbally
informed of the arrangements, but often people who are in turmoil do not readily absorb

all the information they are given and they may become upset and anxious as a result. So when people call to express their sympathies and to enquire when the funeral is to take place, it is amazing how invaluable it is to have the arrangement card propped up beside the telephone to act as a useful prompt.

In the days leading up to the funeral, the funeral director can discuss matters such as hymn sheets, order of service, music to be played (usually something that would have been a favourite of the deceased), are there friends and family who wish to be pall bearers or will the funeral director's staff carry out this duty? Everything must be tailored to the family's needs and wishes. There are no dress rehearsals for a funeral. Things must be exactly right on the day and, as long as it is legal, funeral directors will do everything possible to comply with the wishes of grieving relatives.

Costs

At some stage, funeral costs must be discussed with next-of-kin. If they are reasonably clear about their requirements at the first meeting, it may be appropriate to provide a written estimate of charges, which will also include costs for disbursements that the funeral director expects to pay out on behalf of the family, either before the funeral or on the day itself. These fees, which make up the majority of the cost of a funeral, include those for –

- medical certificates (in the case of cremation)
- grave/grave excavation
- the place of worship
- the religious minister.

Most of these (largely inevitable) costs will be accurately reflected in the estimate but items such as press notices and hymn sheets, for example, cannot be costed until later. The estimate must be signed and dated by the person giving instructions for the funeral, then countersigned by the funeral director, thus forming a legal contract whereby the funeral company will act for and on behalf of the signatory.

It is often helpful if the next-of-kin indicate sooner rather than later that there are financial constraints, as the funeral director can offer advice regarding any monetary help the family may be entitled to. Means-tested state benefits are available to pay for funerals of loved ones and it may be that the family can qualify for financial help.

By law, the funeral director is obliged to make all families aware, regardless of ability to pay, that they offer what is referred to as the Basic Simple Funeral, one that allows for a service at the graveside or in the crematorium chapel only, with no limousines, obituary notices, or use of the funeral home's own chapel beforehand. Where a family chooses this option, a good funeral director will take every bit as much care, will deal just as sensitively with the family, and will ensure the funeral is conducted in a dignified and proper manner, for it is important that those left behind have a good memory of the deceased and feel they have done their best for those they have loved.

What happens in a traditional funeral?

There will have been the opportunity for friends and family to pay their last respects in the chapel of rest prior to the funeral. The day before, the funeral director makes a courtesy visit in person to the family home, so that he can advise that all arrangements have been carried out in accordance with the family's wishes. This is a time for offering reassurance: perhaps a family member is going to do a reading during the religious service or at the crematorium and is by now worrying that he or she will not know when it is time to get up and will move to the front in the wrong place. Little matters like this often cause anxiety. But the funeral director knows about these things and so does the person officiating, so one or other will give a sign when it is time. The courtesy visit also throws up an opportunity for the funeral director to check that no problems have recently arisen: are there road works, temporary traffic lights or anything else that might hinder the progress of the cortege? Satisfied that everything is as it should be, it only remains for the funeral director to assure the family that he will take good care of them on the day.

On the day itself, the vehicles are cleaned, floral tributes are listed, the deceased is checked for jewellery to be removed and returned to the family (though often it is the wish that rings and other jewellery should remain on the body, and if that is the case, the person closing the coffin will do so with a witness present). Once the coffin has been closed, it will be placed in the hearse and flowers will be positioned on top and around it.

Final checks are made, including that the right coffin is on the hearse, the minister's, church's and organist's fees are to hand, the lowering webs for the graveside are clean and on board, and the wheeled bier is in the hearse.

When the hearse arrives at the departure point for the cortege, the funeral director and his staff will ensure that they never appear hurried or flustered, because if they are composed, the family will feel relaxed and confident in their care.

Immediate family will take their seats in the limousine(s), whilst other mourners will follow in their own cars. The cortege then makes its way either to the place where the religious service will take place or to the crematorium. It relies very much on the goodwill of other motorists and for them to accept that a funeral procession cannot and should not be rushed, out of respect for the deceased and the mourners.

On arrival, the funeral director will ensure that everything is in order so that the funeral ceremony can take place. This means placing service sheets in the pews, for example, setting up a CD player where necessary or checking that musicians are ready to play or sing what they have been asked to perform. Finally, he will give instructions to those who will be pall bearers if this task is not being done by his own staff. When the congregation is seated, the coffin will be brought in, possibly to the accompaniment of a favourite piece of music and with the family following close behind. When they are settled and composed in the front pews, the service will begin. If the funeral director has done his work well, the proceedings will move along seamlessly. If he hasn't, family and friends will soon notice.

Committal service

At the end of the service, if the body is to be buried, the congregation will go to the cemetery for the short committal service. If the body is to be cremated, the congregation will proceed to the crematorium where a similarly brief service will also take place, although here, there will be the possibility of singing a final hymn if the family so desires. The cremated remains will be available the following day and the funeral director is often the one who goes to collect them on behalf of the family. If the remains are to be buried, immediate family generally reconvene briefly at the cemetery for the interment. (It is becoming more common for cremation to take place with no mourners present, followed by a full and public service in church, where the casket containing the ashes of the deceased is placed near the altar. The casket is subsequently interred in a cemetery or garden of remembrance.)

After the committal ceremony, either at the cemetery or at the crematorium, it is usual for the family and the rest of the mourners to have some refreshments, though these do not necessarily take place at the home of the next of kin. However, this gathering is a way for everyone to come together one last time after the funeral.

A book of remembrance

Books of remembrance can be found in some, though not all, churches and are situated at most crematoria. When someone is cremated and their remains are not buried in a cemetery with a headstone, there is no "place" where their loved ones can go to remember them. Consequently, an entry in a book of remembrance is a good way for family and friends to have a physical location where they can remember that person's life. You do not have to enter the person's date in the book of remembrance – indeed, crematorium staff will leave it up to you to choose a date that has particular significance. This can be anything from a birthday or wedding anniversary to a date of birth or death. Entries are beautifully inscribed by hand in special script and, for many people, they offer a dignified and permanent memorial to their loved one.

Memorial cards can then be printed which are a copy of the entry in the book of remembrance. They become a keepsake for family and friends and are also useful to send to people who cannot easily visit the crematorium to see the original entry but who nevertheless want to have a physical reminder of the deceased.

Memorial cards ... become a keepsake for family and friends and are also useful to send to people who cannot easily visit the crematorium ...

Memorials

These come in many forms: as well as the book of remembrance, there is the flower receptacle (much like a flower vase), a name plaque, small tablet and, for the cemetery and larger churchyards, headstones.

Regulations now strictly govern memorial size. Gone are the days of big, expensive obelisks. The largest memorials today will be no more than 2ft 6in high by 2ft wide and 4in thick and will be hewn from natural stone. Shapes and colours vary enormously: some have flower holders, others not and it is possible to mount a photographic likeness of your loved one on a ceramic plaque encased in bronze frame on the memorial. Wording of the dedication is subject to approval by the regulatory body, which varies from one area to another. Whereas in the past, dedications were restricted to formal wording, nowadays, there is much more scope for using familiar names and nicknames on headstones and a less formal language is often permitted.

How different religions handle funerals and burial

Every religion has its own way of honouring its dead and of laying the body to rest – whether by burial, cremation or other means.

Roman Catholics signify the approach of death by summoning a priest to hear the dying person's confession and to administer Holy Communion and Extreme Unction, anointing him or her with oil that has been blessed by a bishop, thereby absolving the dying person of guilt. The funeral, normally held in the church that the deceased has regularly attended throughout his or her life, includes a special Eucharist, a Requiem Mass, recalling the last supper that Jesus Christ shared with his disciples before his death. Prayers are said for the dead person's soul and the body in the coffin is blessed with incense and sprinkled with holy water. Catholics are almost always buried, dating back to a belief in the resurrection of the body.

Protestant funeral rites tend to be a simplified version of the Catholic service. The dying person may have a pastor attend the deathbed, at which time prayers are said. A brief prayer is normally said for the deceased at his or her church on the Sunday following the death. The funeral is less formal than the Catholic service, and frequently includes speeches and readings by relatives and close friends. Cremation is common within Protestant communities.

Quaker funerals are informal affairs. The service is one of silent contemplation, broken only when one or more of the people present speak personally about the deceased person or read a poem or text.

Jewish communities have a burial society called a Chevra Kadisha. This is a group of people, many of them volunteers, who prepare the body for burial (cremation is unknown) and help make the funeral arrangements. The burial is usually held within 24 hours of death, though it can be delayed where immediate family members have to travel long distances. The burial service in the cemetery is short. A eulogy (or *hesped*) is given by the rabbi or close family friend, followed by a Kaddish, an ancient prayer, which is recited in Hebrew. The coffin is then taken to the graveside and it is considered an honour to help shovel in the earth.

Muslims are forbidden to cremate their dead, and families try to bury the body within 24 hours of the death. As with Jews, the preparation for a Muslim funeral is only rarely handed over to professionals: family members or close friends normally perform ritual washing of the deceased, with the body wrapped in a shroud of simple, white material. The body is placed in the grave, normally without a coffin, with the face turned right.

Hindu funerals require the body to be cremated. The burning of the body signifies the release of the spirit and the flames represent the presence of the god Brahma, the creator. Prayers are usually said at the entrance to the crematorium. Offerings such as flowers or sweetmeats may be passed around and horns and bells are also part of the ritual. The chief mourner, usually the eldest son or eldest male in the family, represents the whole family in saying goodbye to the deceased. He, and sometimes all the male family members, may shave their heads as a mark of respect. Readings from the scriptures are read, after which the chief mourner pushes the button to make the coffin disappear and, where possible, goes below to ignite the cremator (the equipment used to burn the body). Following the cremation, the family and mourners meet together for a meal and prayers.

Sikhs also use cremation as the traditional method of disposal of the body. The mourners gather at the house of the bereaved family where the body may be on display before departing for the crematorium. Death is seen as an act of the Almighty and there is, therefore, an emphasis on keeping emotions under control, with even family members appearing detached. On the way to the crematorium, hymns may be sung and, once there, prayers may be recited and more hymns sung before the next-of-kin to the deceased presses the button for the coffin to disappear. After the cremation, guests usually return to the family home where there will be more readings and hymns.

Buddhists have few formal traditions relating to funerals, which are seen as non-religious events. Most Buddhist schools of thought see the physical body as a shell and they therefore focus on the spirit or mind of the deceased immediately preceding, and at the time of, death. Buddhists share the Tibetan belief that the spirit of the deceased will be reborn, usually after a period of 49 days. The Buddha himself was cremated – and cremation is generally the accepted practice, with a simple service held at the crematorium chapel at which Buddhist readings are recited.

Humanist funerals acknowledge a loss and celebrate a life, lived by moral principles based on reason and respect for others, with a belief that happiness and fulfilment in this life is all-important. For over a century, the British Humanist Association (BHA) has trained funeral officiants who perform the same task as a vicar or priest, visiting the family to map out the ceremony, frequently in considerable detail to avoid reliance on a standard format – and that creates an accurate and sensitive picture of the deceased person. The service may include favourite music, poetry or prose readings, a tribute to the deceased, along with short contributions from the bereaved, a time of reflection or silent meditation and words of farewell at the burial or cremation.

The humanist service may include favourite music, poetry or prose readings, a tribute to the deceased, along with short contributions from the bereaved, a time of reflection or silent meditation and words of farewell at the burial or cremation.

It is important to know that, if you do not feel comfortable with the first officiant who comes to see you, then you are perfectly entitled to request that another be sent to you instead. If you, the bereaved, do not feel strong enough to insist on this, then get someone else who is more removed from the situation to do it for you. Humanists pride themselves on getting what they say at funerals right, both in terms of tone and content, so they will not mind you requesting this change.

DIY and unconventional funerals and burials

Society is becoming increasingly secular: only half of weddings still take place in church and the same trend is occurring with funerals. There has been a gradual realisation that there are a range of options available over the last two or three decades and that funerals can be personalised, even planned in advance.

In the 1980s, the AIDS epidemic was influential in starting this trend, because many young people faced death, and wished to make their funeral a personalised event and to have time to plan it. The last ten years have seen a rapid increase in the number of natural burial grounds where the body is buried in a biodegradable coffin and the grave is marked by trees, shrubs and wildflowers rather than a headstone.

The BHA now admits that it is unable to satisfy the demand for officiants to lead secular funerals. And to avoid the standardisation and commercialisation of the ceremony, there is a growing trend for do-it-yourself funerals.

There are books that help people who wish to organise their own funerals, as well as companies who will try to satisfy people's growing desire for originality (*see Useful Information pp.188–89*).

There are a number of different aspects to organising a funeral and it should be emphasised that many funeral directors today are aware that relatives want to get involved in planning a funeral – with the best, increasingly, seeing their roles as "enablers", providing expertise while helping their clients to do as much as possible for themselves. The key elements of a funeral to consider range from the choice of casket to songs or texts to be read.

The coffin or casket

There is a growing demand for more upbeat, personalised coffins and caskets, as well as more environmentally friendly ones and companies are stepping in to provide a more customised service that sidesteps the more conventional route. Amongst the most popular alternative options are –

- cardboard, bamboo or willow coffins – all of which are increasingly accepted by crematoria and widely used in natural burial grounds. They can be used with a body bag or lined with hay, sawdust or cotton wool and decorated with water-based paints or crayons. For supplies, contact the Natural Death Centre (*see p.188*).
- coffins that can be used as ordinary furniture until they are needed. Coffins can now be used as anything from beautifully crafted blanket boxes and fully shelved bathroom cabinets to bookcases, long-case clocks and wardrobes. It is also possible to buy a re-usable coffin, a shroud or body bag or even a biodegradable hessian burial stretcher.
- specially strengthened papier-mâché "ecopods", which can be used as biodegradable coffins. Urns for ashes can also be made in a similar way.

Flowers

It is probably best to ignore any meaning when selecting flowers for a funeral: better simply to pick a tribute that you like and that seems appropriate. However, it is worth bearing in mind that particular flowers are associated with death and funerals in different cultures, including –

- white chrysanthemums in Japan, Belgium, Italy and Switzerland
- white asters or carnations in Switzerland
- frangipani blossoms in India
- any yellow flowers in Mexico
- lilies in a variety of cultures – both purple and gold ones, and white ones.

Transport

It is possible to fit a coffin in some estate cars. Otherwise, the options include –

- hiring a car or a hearse from a local funeral director
- hiring a roofed motorcycle sidecar hearse
- hiring a horse-drawn hearse or horse and cart
- hiring a coach. Family and friends can all travel easily to the funeral and burial, and the coffin fits easily in the luggage compartment.

The burial

The Natural Death Centre has drawn up a Good Funeral Guide (incorporated in its Natural Death Handbook), based on its survey of 800 cemeteries and listed according to price and how far a personalised burial is permitted.

Green funerals

Natural burial grounds are now sited throughout the UK and in many other countries. The burial takes place in a biodegradable coffin or shroud, and a tree, shrub or wildflowers are planted instead of having a headstone. The Association of Natural Burial Grounds (c/o the Natural Death Centre) has a code of practice guaranteeing long-term security of both the graves and the wildlife, the keeping of a permanent record of all graves as well as fair and reasonable charges.

It is possible to bury someone under a tree in your garden or on farmland, provided the grave is on dry land and away from watercourses and gas and electricity services to avoid the danger of pollution or the possibility of severing pipes or cables. Even burial at sea, though rare, is a possibility, as long as certain regulations are adhered to (burials are carried out in designated areas where the tides will not return the body back to shore). If the body is cremated, the ashes can be disposed of anywhere in the world, or, indeed, in space.

Psychotherapist Josefine Speyer recalls her adult son spending an afternoon digging his father's grave at a family-organised green funeral. *'It was a very satisfying physical contribution for my son and his friends. It was a part of an emotional journey that gave him a sense of ownership,'* she recalls. *'Afterwards everyone helped to fill the grave and those invited recounted memories, read poetry or played music. There was a feeling of empowerment, a sense of belonging, of people making a worthwhile contribution.'*

The officiant or celebrant

This can be a minister of religion, a non-religious celebrant or officiant or even a friend or relative. It is not an easy task to carry out, though, and requires someone who can retain their composure throughout the ceremony.

The service

A suggested structure for a funeral ceremony includes music, readings of prose and poetry, with thoughts on the meaning and value of a life and the inevitability of death, along with tributes, a eulogy and readings from letters and poetry by family members.

Poetry and texts

Funerals without God (published by the BHA) has an excellent selection of poetry by Christina Rossetti (*When I am dead, my dearest/Sing no sad songs for me*); Robert Louis Stevenson *(Home is the sailor, home from sea/and the hunter home from the hill)*; Shelley *(He is a portion of the loveliness which once he made more lovely)*; Shakespeare *(Fear no more the heat of the sun/Nor the furious winter's rages;/Thou thy worldly task hast done/Home art gone and ta'en thy wages)*; George Eliot, Thomas Hardy and A.E. Housman are also good sources. The British Humanist Association's book, *Funerals Without God* also has a selection of texts and turns of phrases for use in –

- the opening words
- thoughts on life and death
- the tribute to the deceased
- the committal
- the closing words.

Poet Laureate, Andrew Motion, has produced an inspiring and supportive booklet entitled: *Well Chosen Words: How to Write a Eulogy*, available free from Cooperative Funeralcare (*see p.188*).

Music

Make your own CD, either recording it yourself or getting help to compile a special funeral CD (*see pp.188–89*). The top ten funeral songs, all secular, according to the *Guardian* newspaper, are –

1 *My Way* by Frank Sinatra
2 *I will always love you* by Whitney Houston

3 *Unchained Melody* by the Righteous Brothers
4 *Wind Beneath My Wings* by Bette Midler
5 *Memories* by Barbra Streisand
6 *Imagine* by John Lennon
7 *In the Mood* by Glenn Miller
8 *Walking in the Air* by Aled Jones
9 *Wonderful World* by Louis Armstrong
10 *Smoke Gets in your Eyes*

A relative or friend singing live or playing a much-loved tune can be the perfect option. An alternative is to hire a singer and/or musicians.

- The British Humanist Association is starting to make a list of musicians willing to do this work. Its book, *Funeral without God*, includes a handful of suitable excerpts from classical music by Chopin, Mozart, Elgar and Mendelssohn.
- Contact the Musicians Union or a local arts centre, school or university to track down local musicians prepared to undertake this work.
- Some larger firms of undertakers can also call on the services of musicians and singers who will perform at funeral services.
- Jazz bands can also be hired: anything from a solo saxophonist to a full eight-piece band (*see pp.188–89*).

The memorial service

Memorial services were traditionally a rare event in bereavement: a signal that a terrible tragedy had occurred or that the deceased was one of the great and the good. However, all this is changing. There is a growing recognition of the value of friends and family meeting together beyond the funeral to celebrate the death of a loved one, rather than simply mark it.

The actor, Annabel Leventon, has helped to organise a number of memorial events for fellow performers and says the harder you work at them, the more you get back. "It's about creating a community that is gathered together with the sole purpose of celebrating one life. The first time, I was asked to do something for the principal of my drama school.

Instead of just singing a song, I decided to get the whole of my year together and we all sang together in close part harmony, something lots of us were not very good at. It really re-activated the spirit of what it was like to be students again, striving for excellence under his inspirational lead. For me, organising something is a way through grief partly because it's helping others."

Whether it is a gathering of friends and family who meet for afternoon tea and talk about their memories, a ceremony to scatter the ashes, or an event on a far more splendid scale, the memorial gathering is an important ritual, because it enables people to pray for, remember and celebrate the dead person. It can be an important part of grieving, in that it helps those close to the dead person to become a community that has a shared knowledge and love of the deceased – even if it is only for a few hours. A memorial service has the added benefit that it can be organised as long as you want after the person's death, and to suit those who might attend. Sometimes, people arrange a funeral for immediate family and friends in the place where the deceased is to be buried or cremated, then a memorial service in another part of the country (or indeed in another country) where the deceased also had strong ties. As with funerals, so with memorial services nowadays: (almost) anything goes, and funeral directors are happy to help arrange memorials. Alternatively, you can design and organise the entire gathering yourself.

… the memorial gathering is an important ritual, because it enables people to pray for, remember and celebrate the dead person.

Memorials can also be things, not services. The family can either keep an object that belonged to the dead person or give money, for example, for a special memorial seat, garden or tree. The permanent physical nature of such memorials helps people to see death as part of everyday life, helps them to grieve and helps them to keep the deceased loved one present in their thoughts. When the memorial has a practical element to it – whether it be a charitable trust set up in that person's name, or simply a park bench that people can use in years to come – it can help those left behind to see that that person's life, through death, continues to have a purpose, and this too helps the grieving process.

Chapter 6 **Planning for your death**

Death is sometimes described as a being a taboo subject. Perhaps it's more a case that, with most people living to an advanced age, death is no longer in the midst of everyday life and many people are well into adulthood before they ever have to face the death of a close friend or family member. There is no reason to believe that, as a society, we are any more in denial about death than we used to be. It is simply that we are more ignorant about it because we come across it so much less.

All of which means that people today may have to make a little bit more effort, not just to prepare for the inevitable, but also to face up to their own mortality and to live accordingly. Far from being a depressing activity, facing up to, and preparing for an event that happens to everybody, can be both calming and life-enhancing.

Preparing for your death

Planning in advance for your own death should include taking practical steps to avoid leaving those you love to sort out the mess afterwards. That includes writing a will and ensuring your papers are in order as well as considering the preparation of an Advance Directive to give doctors an idea of how you would like to be treated, should you lose the power to give consent directly. There is also now the opportunity to appoint an attorney to administer your estate in such a situation.

Thinking and talking about dying in a practical sort of way can help to break down taboos that still exist in some families. It can bring people together, help the younger generation to feel secure and cared for, as well as allow each of us to be creative and prepare memories for our loved ones, thereby enabling us to have an influence on the way that others remember us.

Thinking and talking about dying in a practical sort of way can help to break down taboos that still exist in some families.

Planning for dying can also be an opportunity for emotional and spiritual development. "Death and the sun are not to be looked at steadily," wrote the 17th-century French writer, La Rochefoucauld. However, in the same way that sunlight makes us grow, the first close bereavement brings a growth in maturity to many people. We realise we are not immortal, that our time is finite, and this realisation can give us the motivation and the wisdom to make the most of our lives, to communicate with our nearest and dearest and to tell them that we love them. Paradoxically, if bereavement happens in middle age, and particularly if it is due to the death of our parents, this sudden awareness of mortality and of the fact that we are "next in line" in the natural order of things can cause a double sense of urgency and can be positively enriching.

Sorting out the mess: an agenda for action

Imagine what it would be like if a tragic combination of events caused you to lose, and forget everything about, all your personal details: your bank account number, your email address and where you kept your passport, your travel card or your car keys. And imagine that this same tragic course of events led you to forget the names and contact details of your friends, colleagues and relatives – both those close to you and those that are now remote but were at one time very special.

It is precisely this situation that frequently faces an executor or relative dealing with the affairs of a deceased person: both immediately after the death as the funeral is being prepared and later, when someone has to make decisions about the disposal of property, check on insurance policies, the state of the mortgage and any other bills and payments that are needed – and even know where to cancel the milk.

To protect your loved ones from having to sort through this kind of mess is easy. All you have to do is get a file or two and fill it with all the information that underpins your life. Give yourself plenty of time to do it.

Alternatively, get some help from an organisation that knows what it is talking about. You can order Age Concern's excellent eight-page leaflet, *Instructions For My Next of Kin and Executors upon my Death* (*see p.189 for contact details*), which collects together the information that you can put together in a couple of hours or, perhaps, an afternoon, but which would probably prove an impossible task for anyone else.

It begins with straightforward personal details including the name of the solicitor, accountant, bank, tax inspector and pension advisor as well as details of insurance policies and insurance company contacts. It provides instructions on where to find the will, a list of people who should be contacted following the death and the name and contact details of the person who will make arrangements for the funeral. You can leave instructions on where to find house keys, birth and marriage certificates, passport, deeds of the house, lease of the property, mortgage and hire purchase agreements, along with credit cards, premium bond certificates, income tax papers, computer password, email addresses, mobile phone number and car keys – even the names and addresses of who should be invited to your funeral and how to cancel newspapers and milk delivery.

Tell your story

It is not just practical information that can make a difference to those you leave behind. Leaving letters for loved ones, sorting family photographs or putting together a collection of family history can be meaningful, not just for those left behind, but for their children and grandchildren.

You could go further, with a tape-recorded or videoed message specifically intended to be shown after your death. The best time to do it could be straight away. Nicholas Albery, the co-founder of the Natural Death Centre (*see p.189*), recorded a video message for posterity at the age of 50, just three years before his tragic death in a car accident. It was a relaxed, informal recording by a film-maker friend, with Albery speaking about what he believed the afterlife would be like and what he felt was important in life. He passed on bits of wisdom and advice with characteristic humour, while avoiding speaking of his regrets (with the exception of advising: "Don't send your children to public school"). It was played repeatedly at his memorial service, turning it into a unique event.

Maxine Edginton was terminally ill with cancer when she had her story turned into the song, *We Laughed,* by singer Billy Bragg. She saw it make number 11 in the charts in November 2005. The song is based on a photograph of Maxine and her 15-year-old daughter, taken shortly after she had been given six months to live at the end of 2004. *"I just wrote lots of things that had meaning to me and the experience somehow allowed me to release my innermost feelings. I realised that dying is not actually about me, it's about those around me, their feelings, their needs, their ability to cope and their knowing that I love them. It's about leaving nothing unsaid, preparing them for my departure but leaving happy memories of our last days together. I tried to make each day one in which we would remember the laughter more than the sadness and it gave me great comfort to know that I was doing the right thing both for Jessica and for myself,"* Maxine wrote in her website (see p.189).

A diagnosis of terminal illness may bring out a latent creativity, amid the turmoil. That view has been most extensively promoted by Elisabeth Kübler-Ross, an American psychiatrist who died in 2004, and who had devoted her working life to caring for, and speaking on behalf of, the terminally ill. One of her many books, *Death – The Final Stage of Growth*, sums up her belief in the potential for "living well before dying well", and in the opportunity for many people to discover truths about themselves in their final weeks of life, as "the grim reality of death forces us to break through the façade behind which we have hidden not only ourselves from others but also from ourselves".

Today, a number of hospices run creative workshops to help people at the end of their lives to write their stories. Rosetta Life is a charity that provides trained artists, film-makers, poets, song-writers and musicians to work on a one-to-one basis with hospice patients, enabling them to explore different mediums including digital art, poetry, photography and even opera in order that they may find a voice and rediscover themselves at the very moment when they may feel most lost. This creative process can be healing, as working through the arts helps people facing long-term illness to recover the confidence and self-esteem that illness so often takes away.

In the months before Sally Mijit's artist husband, Akbar, died of cancer at a London hospice, his energy was at an all-time low, she recalls. *"It's so easy to become institutionalised, to focus only on the next meal, the next blood-pressure reading. By working with artists in the hospice, Rosetta Life brought something quite different into our lives."* Though suffering from peripheral neuropathy and barely able to move his hands, Akbar started to paint vibrant red and yellow flames. *"It's wonderful to have them, to know that he was so positive, so productive at the end of his life,"* she says.

Several hundred people have already had the Rosetta Life experience and thousands more are able to benefit from the results, many of which are accessible via the website (*see p.189*). Perhaps its most important message, however, is the capacity for creative self-expression among those with life-threatening illness, whether they have access to this support service or not.

Writing a will

Three out of four people under the age of 45 and half of all those aged over 45, fail to make a will. Those who go on to die intestate bequeath financial and organisational problems to relatives and a potential field day for lawyers. The net result usually means worry and stress for those left behind, and often a few unpleasant surprises as well.

After losing first his mother then his brother (to prostate cancer), Ian continues to live in the family home. *"I am still suffering from the Inland Revenue 'sniffing' into my bank accounts as my brother sadly left a mess with his financial affairs as a result of his illness. I hope my experience will convince people to write a will to avoid further distress and allow close relatives and executors to get on with living."*

There may also be uncertainty over who will take care of children or other dependants, notably if the parents are not married. And where partners have been married more than once, with children from different marriages and where there are a number of dependants, the absence of a will can cause particular complications.

The most basic consequence of dying intestate is that you do not keep control over what happens to your savings and property. It may be that the people who are important to you will end up with a fair share of your estate. If that is the case, it will be happy coincidence. The chances are that the lawyers will be the ones to benefit the most, while your property will quite possibly end up with people whom you did not intend to pass it on to.

Exactly why so many people fail to write a will is not clear. Is it because of chronic procrastination and an irrational belief that life will go on forever, or is it because it is seen as an unnecessary expense?

If it is the latter, the way forward is worth careful consideration. Though will-writing doesn't have to be expensive, most experts advise that it is unwise to cut corners. Buying a kit from a stationer and writing it without expert advice is the cheapest option. But there is considerable potential for making mistakes that cannot be corrected. Age Concern offers a will-writing service that allows you to have your will written for a modest sum of money by a qualified and highly experienced solicitor. This is an ideal option for anyone whose circumstances are relatively straightforward.

The Law Society, however, recommends sitting down with an expert, preferably a solicitor with a specialist interest in the subject, for a face-to-face discussion in preparing the will. In so doing, the solicitor can take account of your circumstances and alert you to the potential consequences of anything you wish to do before you make a final decision that is then irreversible. Although anyone can draw up a legal document, a specially trained solicitor is more likely to be able to draw up a document that cannot be misinterpreted and that everyone can understand.

How to choose a solicitor

The best method is to go by personal recommendation. Otherwise, the Law Society has a list of solicitors with a particular interest in wills. Call the Law Society or visit them online (see p.189) and search under Wills and Probate to get details of solicitors in your area. Charges for drawing up a will vary between solicitors and depend on the experience of the solicitor and how complicated the will may be. If possible, speak to four or five solicitors before making an appointment. As well as price, try to find someone who is approachable and a good communicator.

7 extra reasons to write a will

1. You are not married to your partner

2. You have children or dependants who may not be able to care for themselves

3. There is an issue of inheritance tax

4. Several people could make a claim on your estate when you die because they depend on you financially

5. Your permanent home is not in the UK or you are not a British citizen

6. You live here but have overseas property

7. You own all or part of a business

1 reason to update your will

1. You have married, separated, divorced, had a child, moved house or experienced another major life change. Major changes are best dealt with by drawing up a new will, though minor changes can be made to an existing will as codicils. The Law Society recommends reviewing the will at least every five years.

What do you need to know to write a will?

In order to write a will, you will need to list the following details –

- What you own: property, cars, personal valuables, stocks and shares, bank accounts, insurance policies, businesses and pensions.
- An idea of how you want to divide your property between relatives, friends or charities – and any conditions you want to attach to these gifts.
- Details of your family and married status. Remember that anyone who depends on you financially can ask a court to review your will if they feel you have not provided properly for them. By explaining all relevant information to your solicitor, he or she can highlight any legal pitfalls.
- The name of one or more legal guardians of any children who may still be under 18 when you die.

- Whether you are registered as an organ donor.
- The people who you wish to appoint as executors of your will and who will carry out the administration of your will after your death.
- Any particular wishes for your funeral: do you wish to be buried or cremated and do you wish to have a religious or non-religious funeral?
- Do you prefer money to be given to a specific charity, rather than have floral tributes at the funeral?

Many people are clear about the sort of funeral they want and make sure they write down in advance precise details of the ceremony and burial, especially if they do not want these to be along traditional lines. Some go as far as buying unconventional coffins and caskets in advance (*see pp.188–89 for information on companies which provide these*) but most simply want those left behind to be quite clear about what sort of "send off" that person wished to have.

"Everyone at my funeral is to bring daffodil bulbs, and then they would be planted in a BIG smile on Goodwood Hill. I won't half have to work hard to make new friends and influence people, won't I, with a smile that big!" Beryl, 67, makes her wishes known for her funeral.

Pre-paid Funeral Plans

Some people opt for a "Pre-paid Funeral Plan". These are often taken out many years before death is likely to occur, partly for financial reasons: funeral costs, which include local authority charges, doctor's, religious service and minister's fees, as well as those of the funeral director, go up annually. By taking out a pre-paid plan, people feel that matters relating to their funeral will be easier for those left behind and this provides them with peace of mind. In addition, these plans can avoid the family feeling guilty about how much it feels should be spent on the funeral if much of it has been paid for in advance. Finally, the wishes of the deceased have already been clarified in terms of what sort of funeral and burial they would like and that too is often a comfort to grieving relatives.

Who should you appoint as executors of your will?

- They can be friends or family members or a professional such as your solicitor. The Law Society suggests that a good combination would be a friend or family member and a professional such as a solicitor, especially where there are large investments to administer.

- It is a good idea to choose someone who is familiar with your financial matters.
- It is advisable to pick someone who is younger than you.
- Always ensure that the people you choose are happy to take on the duty, which includes both dealing with day-to-day matters to do with your home, and the long-term business of administering your estate.

Who should you appoint as guardians?

- The most common choice is to appoint family members, particularly where very young children are concerned.
- As children grow older, it may be more appropriate to appoint friends who live nearby and share your lifestyle.
- It is normally best to appoint two partners who live together, rather than a "committee" of single relatives. In this way, children get the chance to become part of a stable environment at the most difficult time in their lives.

Once the will has been written, it needs to be signed by two witnesses and kept safely, either at home or with a solicitor or bank.

Letter of wishes

As well as making a will, you can also prepare a "letter of wishes" to give away personal effects and other small items and where you can make requests of your executors. You may also wish to write an informal letter to the guardians to give an indication of the way, for instance, that you would wish your child or children to be brought up, though the Law Society advises against trying to enforce too rigid a routine either in the letter or in the will, in order to avoid making the guardian's job harder by trying to impose out-of-date attitudes. Many people have very specific and clear ideas about what they want to put in the will. But you should be cautious, however tempting it might be, about trying to rule beyond the grave. There should always be a degree of flexibility available to the executors so that they are able to deal with matters that have not been anticipated. However, if you have appointed guardians and executors that you trust implicitly to do the right thing, the need will hopefully not arise to try to control the situation down to the last detail.

Drawing up an Advance Statement for your doctors

Most people who are ill today expect to discuss treatment options with their doctor and jointly reach a decision about any future treatment. As a mentally competent adult, you cannot be given medical treatment unless you give your consent.

But what happens if you are admitted to hospital when you are unconscious or unable to talk? What if your mental health deteriorates to the extent that you are unable to process information and understand the implications of the treatment that is being proposed, which could happen as a result of having a stroke or through developing a form of dementia?

In such a situation, you are not considered competent to participate in making a decision about your treatment because you "lack mental capacity". Doctors have a legal and ethical obligation to act in your best interests at all times. And British Medical Association guidance states that it is good practice for doctors to consult with relatives in order to determine your best interests. However, relatives do not have a legal right to be consulted or to make decisions on your behalf.

For all these reasons, it is now widely accepted that it is helpful for doctors to have a copy of written information that reflects your views and wishes should you reach a stage where you lack mental capacity to give consent. And there are a number of different ways in which you can do this.

An Advance Statement is a general statement indicating your preference as to what form of medical treatment you would or would not like to receive, in the event that you are unable to decide or communicate your wishes for yourself. In the statement, you may also nominate someone whom you wish to be consulted at a time that a decision has to be made.

The aim of the Advance Statement is to inform the doctors who are caring for you. It does not bind them to a particular course of action and there is no obligation for them to follow your wishes if it conflicts with their professional judgement.

What is an Advance Directive or Living Will?

This is a legally binding document that gives you a chance to indicate your future wishes at a time when you are able to make decisions for yourself. It gives you the same rights that you have as a competent adult in a situation where you have lost the capacity to make such a decision.

All competent adults are entitled to refuse treatment for any reason, rational or irrational, even if this might lead to their death. However, no one in the UK is able to insist that a particular medical treatment is given to them. Thus, an Advance Directive can only be a refusal of treatment and is a statement indicating –

- your specific wish to refuse all or some forms of medical treatment
- the circumstances under which this refusal would apply.

The Advance Directive must be prepared at a time that you are mentally capable and takes effect only when you have lost the capacity to participate in the decision-making process.

An Advance Directive or Living Will does not have to be in writing. It can be information provided in a verbal discussion, though a verbal Advance Directive will normally only be taken seriously if the discussion is between the patient and a senior member of the medical team. A casual remark to a friend or relative does not count as an Advance Directive.

It is increasingly becoming the norm for doctors to raise the subject of treatment options at an early stage, for instance, when they are first discussing a terminal diagnosis with the patient. Relatives frequently find it a relief to know that they will not have to make these decisions themselves at what is likely to be a stressful time later on.

Beresford recalls the time when his mother, aged 92, was admitted to a small, local hospital, with a heart attack: *"On arrival, my mother explained that she was a Christian Scientist and did not believe in medical help. At that point, the hospital said that they were not prepared to do 'nothing', as my mother had had a heart attack and would need treatment. She would therefore be transferred to a larger general hospital in the area. The communication between the two hospitals was good. The larger hospital was warned that my mother was being transferred and did not want any treatment for her heart attack. She was 92 years old and did not have a doctor or medical records. She was told what was going to happen, and that her children were being contacted and would be advised of the situation. The medical staff explained to me that my mother had insisted that they were not to give her any treatment whatsoever. It was explained to me that she would therefore die within a few days. She would only receive food and water. Her physical needs were taken care of, and the staff were most kind and gentle with her. She was transferred back to her local hospital shortly before she died. She was not resuscitated, and the medical staff were most understanding to my mother and all her family. We arrived in the ward just a few moments after she had passed away. The nurse told us that she was holding my mother's hand and that, as she went, she looked like a happy 21 year-old. All the lines on her face had disappeared, something she said she had not seen before. I won't forget that. She died a wonderful, peaceful death."*

When is the best time to make an Advance Statement or Directive?

- Now, if you have strong feelings about a particular situation that could arise in the future.
- As soon as possible after a diagnosis of a terminal illness or a form of dementia. Your doctor can help you understand the consequences of refusing or opting for a particular treatment and relate specific decisions to the likely course of treatment. If you have already written an Advance Statement or Directive, it is probably sensible to rewrite it at this point.
- Whenever it is written, it needs to be updated regularly. Doctors are likely to discount a statement that has been written many years previously, and may only consider a directive that is clearly referring to the actual situation that has arisen.

An Advance Directive cannot –

- ask for anything that is illegal such as euthanasia or for help to commit suicide

- demand care that the health team considers inappropriate in your case

- refuse the offer of food and drink by mouth

- refuse the use of measures solely designed to maintain your comfort, such as providing appropriate pain relief

- refuse basic nursing care that is essential to keep you comfortable, such as washing, bathing and mouth care

If you choose to draft your own Advance Statement and/or Advance Directive, the minimum information you need to include is –

- full name
- address
- name, address and telephone number of GP
- whether advice was sought from a health care professional

- date
- signature
- dated signature of at least one witness over the age of 18 years who should not be a partner, spouse, relative or anyone else who stands to benefit under your ordinary will. The witness should not be your health care proxy
- a clear statement of your wishes and values
- if applicable, the name, address and telephone number of the person you have nominated to be consulted about treatment decisions and, preferably, a dated signature that they have agreed to do so and have discussed your wishes with you
- where relevant, the date that you reviewed and, if necessary, revised your Advance Statement with your signature.

(*See pp.182–83 for more information on Advance Statements, Advance Directives and Living Wills.*)

Making an Enduring Power of Attorney

If you have property, savings, investments or any other income, it is sensible to make an Enduring Power of Attorney (EPA). This involves appointing one or more people as your attorney, to look after your financial interests at a time when you are unable to do so.

This can be done on a temporary basis – for instance, if you are away on holiday or in hospital. The attorney(s) that you appoint can use your finances to buy essentials on your behalf – such as food or payment of regular bills. Failure to do this can lead to considerable problems.

> *"I found the pension people most unhelpful. I needed to get my mum's money from the day she went into hospital. When they phoned up for permission, the hospital was told my mum had to be 'assessed', which would take about ten days. I needed the money to pay my mum's rent and bills. All the other members of the family had to help. My mum would not have wished for this."* Susan, on the financial problems she faced when her mother was suddenly hospitalised following a massive stroke that left her in a coma.

The EPA can become a permanent arrangement at a time when you lose the physical or mental capacity to look after your own financial interests. At this point, the attorney or attorneys can apply to the Public Guardianship Office, an office of the Supreme Court with a function to protect the finances and property of people who are mentally incapable of dealing with their own affairs. At that point, the attorney(s) are able to take over the management of your affairs permanently – even to the point of deciding to sell your house, if that is seen as being in your best interests.

The attorney(s) have no power to decide where you live or what kind of medical treatment you receive. But making this kind of arrangement can make it easier for those caring for you, should you lose mental capacity to manage your affairs.

How to set up an EPA

- If you are considering making an EPA it is advisable to seek independent legal advice from a solicitor (see p.178 on Law Society).

- An EPA must be made on a specific form available from a solicitor or law stationers. Ensure that an up-to-date form is used and that it is completed correctly, or it will not be valid. Your solicitor can advise you on this.

- It must then be signed by the attorney and witnessed. The attorney must sign the form before the donor becomes mentally incapable. The attorney may not act as witness.

- If the original document is held by an attorney or lodged with a solicitor or a bank, you should keep a copy for yourself. The solicitor can provide certified copies of the document.

- It may help to avoid later misunderstandings if you call a family conference to explain your reasons for making an EPA.

Becoming an organ donor

Organ transplantation is one of the success stories of modern medicine. Every year, the lives of around 3,000 people are saved or dramatically improved by having a transplanted organ: the majority of them kidneys, but also hearts, lungs, livers and corneas. But they depend entirely on donors and their families being prepared to make this life-saving gift. There is no automatic assumption in the UK that everyone wants to be a donor after their death, as happens in many European countries, and organ donation remains an entirely voluntary opt-in system. And while 90 per cent of the UK population says they would be willing to donate their organs after their death, only around 12,800,000 people, around 21 per cent of the population, have actually joined the NHS Organ Donor Register. As a consequence, 400 people die waiting for a transplant and thousands more suffer chronic ill-health unnecessarily.

In his book, *Dealing Creatively With Death*, Ernest Morgan proposes that his deathbed becomes "the Bed of Life" as his body is taken from it to help others lead fuller lives: *"Give my sight to the man who has never seen a sunrise, a baby's face or love in the eyes of a woman. Give my heart to the person whose own heart has caused nothing but endless days of pain. Give my kidneys to a person who depends upon a machine to exist from week to week. Take my bones, every muscle, every fibre and nerve in my body and find a way to make a crippled child walk. Take my cells, if necessary, and let them grow so that, someday, a speechless boy will shout at the crack of a bat or a deaf girl will hear the sound of rain against the window. If by chance you wish to remember me, do it with a kind deed or word to someone who needs you. If you do all I have asked, I will live forever."*

You can carry a donor card. Far better, however, is to become a registered organ donor by joining the NHS Organ Donor Register (*see p.189 for more information*). Even if you have registered as a donor, it is essential to discuss your decision with your family, as the relatives of a deceased person are always asked to approve organ donation even when the person is registered.

Useful information

Chapter 1

Cancer BACUP Charity that helps people living with cancer. Freephone UK
helpline: 0808 800 1234, www.cancerbacup.org.uk
Irish Cancer Society www.cancer.ie

Chapter 3

Macmillan's Carer Support Group Macmillan Cancer freephone
helpline: 0808 808 2020,   www.macmillan.org.uk
Liverpool Care Pathway www.lcp-mariecurie.org.uk
Preferred Place of Care Plan www.cancerlancashire.org.uk/ppc
Gold Standards Framework www.goldstandardsframework.nhs.uk

Chapter 4

Cruse Bereavement Care Tel: 0870 1671677, www.crusebereavementcare.org.uk
The Way Foundation Support for those bereaved before 50. Tel: 0870 0113450,
www.wayfoundation.org.uk
Child Bereavement Trust UK charity that provides information and support
for bereaved children and families. Information and support line: 0845 357 1000,
www.childbereavement.org.uk
Compassionate Friends Charity that supports bereaved parents and their
families. Helpline: 08451 23 23 04, www.tcf.org.uk
The Bereavement Counselling Service www.bereavementireland.org

Chapter 5

Association of Natural Burial Grounds c/o the Natural Death Centre.
Tel: 020 7359 8391www.naturaldeath.org.uk
Also *How to Organise a Natural or DIY Funeral* (email booklet).
British Humanist Association Tel: 020 7079 3580/ 020 7430 0908,
www.humanism.org.uk
Cooperative Funeralcare Tel : 0800 083 6301, www.funeralcare.co-op.co.uk

Choosing an officiant for a funeral

Choice Farewells   Tel: 02380 861256, www.choiceceremonies.co.uk

ARKA Original Funerals   Tel: 01273 766620, www.eco-funerals.com

The Association of Interfaith Ministers & Spiritual Counsellors
www.interfaithministers.org.uk

Chapter 6

Age Concern   FREEPOST SWB 30375, Ashburton, Devon, TQ13 7ZZ
Tel: 0800 009966, www.ageconcern.org.uk

The Law Society   Tel: 0870 606 6575, www.solicitors-online.com

Maxine Edginton   www.maxiedginton.co.uk

Natural Death Centre   Tel: 020 7359 8391, www.naturaldeath.org.uk

Rosetta Life   www.rosettarequiem.org

Advance Statements, Advance Directives and Living Wills

Age Concern Information sheet IS5, available free, tel: 0800 009966 or
www.ageconcern.org.uk/AgeConcern/information-170/htm

Alzheimer's Society   Information sheet 464, available free, tel: 0845 300 0336 or
www.Alzheimers.org.uk Free information sheet and guidance on preparing an
Advance Directive.

Department of Constitutional Affairs Selborne House, Victoria Street, London,
SW1E 6QW. *Making Decisions: a guide for family and friends*. Booklet available from
www.dca.gov.uk/capacity/index.htm, under "information booklets".

Patients' Association   PO Box, Harrow, Middx, HA1 3YJ.
Helpline : 0845 608 4455. Produces booklet : *Living Wills – a guide for patients* or
from www.patients-association.com

MIND Tel: 0845 766 0163, www.mind.org.uk Free information sheet: *Advance Directives*

Summary of Mental Incapacity Act 2005   Request a copy from Mental
Incapacity Team. Tel : 020 7210 8337, or www.dca.gov.uk/menincap/legis.htm.

How to register as an organ donor

NHS Organ Donor Line   Tel: 0845 60 60 400 (lines open 7am–11pm except
Christmas Day and New Year's Day) or join online at www.uktransplant.org.uk

Index

abc

def

ghij

References/sources

Chapter 1

David Kessler *The Rights of the Dying* (HarperPerennial, 1998)

Lynn J, Adamson DM. *Living well at the end of life. Adapting health care to serious chronic illness in old age.* RAND Health. USA. 2003

Davies E and Higginson IJ, Eds. *The Solid Facts. Palliative Care* (World Health Organization, 2004)

Doyle D, Hanks G, Cherny N and Calman K, eds. *Oxford Textbook of Palliative Medicine 3rd Ed.* (Oxford University Press, 2004)

Ellershaw J and Wilkinson S, Eds. *Care of the Dying. A Pathway to Excellence* (Oxford University Press, 2003)

Twycross R, *Introducing Palliative Care 4th ed.* (Radcliffe Medical Press Ltd, 2003)

Cancer Survival: England 1998-2003 (www.statistics.gov.uk/statbase/Product.asp?vlnk=14007)

Deaths by age, sex and underlying cause, 2004 registration: Health Statistics Quarterly 26 (www.statistics.gov.uk/STATBASE/ssdataset.asp?vlnk=8986)

Clinical Guidelines Working Party. *Changing Gear: Guidelines for Managing the Last Days of Life – 1997* (National Council for Hospice and Specialist Palliative Care Services, December 1997)

Coping with advanced cancer and *Dying with cancer.* Cancer BACUP, helping people live with cancer (www.cancerbacup.org.uk/Resourcessupport/Advancedcancer/)

Chapter 2

C.S. Lewis *A Grief Observed* (Faber paperbacks)

Chapter 3

Ellershaw J E, Murphy D, Shea T, Foster A, Overill S, *Development of a multiprofessional care pathway for the dying patient* (European Journal of Palliative Care 1997;4(6):203-208)

Ellershaw J E, Ward C, *Care of the dying patient: the last hours or days of life* (BMJ 2003 Jan 4; 326(7379):30-4)

The NHS Cancer Plan – A plan for investment, A plan for reform (2000, Department of Health)

National Institute for Clinical Excellence *Guidance on Cancer Services – Improving Supportive and Palliative Care for Adults with Cancer. The Manual* (NICE, March 2004)

John Diamond *C : Because Cowards Get Cancer Too* (Vermilion, 1999)

Joan Didion *The Year of Magical Thinking* (Fourth Estate, 2005)

Elisabeth Kübler-Ross *On Death and Dying* (Prentice Hall, 1997)

Chapter 4

Rebecca Abrams *When Parents Die* (Routledge, 1999)

Michael Harrington *The Other America* (1962)

Virginia Ironside *You'll Get Over It* (Penguin, 1997)

Jessica Mitford *The American Way of Death* (1963)

John Morgan *Death and Bereavement Around the World* (Baywood Publishing, 2004)

Rabbi Julia Neuberger *Dying Well* (Radcliffe Medical Press, 2004)

Chapter 5

Virginia Ironside *You'll Get Over It* (Penguin, 1997)

Elisabeth Kübler-Ross *Death – The Final Stage of Growth* (Touchstone, 1997)

John Morgan *Death and Bereavement Around the World* (Baywood Publishing, 2004)

Rabbi Julia *Neuberger Dying Well* (Radcliffe Medical Press, 2004)

Dr Tony Walter *Funerals and How to Improve Them* (Hodder & Stoughton, 1990)

Cooperative Funeralcare *Well Chosen Words: How to Write a Eulogy* by Andrew Motion (available free, tel: 0800 083 6301, www.funeralcare.co-op.co.uk)

The Natural Death Centre *The Natural Death Handbook,* edited by Stephanie Wienrich and Josefine Speyer (Rider Books)

The Natural Death Centre *How to Organise a Natural or DIY Funeral* (email booklet)

Jane Wynne Wilson *Funerals Without God* (British Humanist Association)

Jean Francis Time to Go, *Alternative Funerals : the Importance of Saying Goodbye* (I Universe)

Sue Gill and John Fox *Dead Good Funerals* (Welfare State International, Ulverston, Cumbria, 1996)

Chapter 6

Keven Kendrick and Simon Robinson *Their Rights: Advance Directives and Living Wills* (Age Concern, 2002), tel: 0870 4422120

Ernest Morgan *Dealing Creatively with Death* (Upper Access, 2001)